BELLWETHER BLUES

A CONSERVATIVE AWAKENING OF
THE MILLENNIAL SOUL

JONATHAN R JAKUBOWSKI

Ballast Books, LLC
Washington, DC
www.ballastbooks.com

ISBN 978-1-7334280-2-6

Library of Congress Control Number has been applied for

Printed in Canada

Published by Ballast Books
www.ballastbooks.com

For more information, bulk orders, appearances or speaking requests,
please email info@ballastbooks.com

Our Father in Heaven, Hallowed be Your Name

*To Missy, who encouraged me to complete this book
while patiently enduring many hours of writing
during weekends, early mornings, and late nights.*

*And for Emelia, Judah, Samuel, and Levi.
As much as this book is written for others,
I pray that I can embody its values in our home.*

*And for my extended family and friends.
Your prayers and support are like oxygen to the lungs.*

*And for the seven courageous individuals
who were willing to share their stories.
Your stories make this book worth reading.*

BELLWETHER BLUES:
A Conservative Awakening in the Millennial Soul

Foreword 7

Preface 11

PART 1: Setting the Stage

Chapter 1: The Millennial Dilemma .17

Chapter 2: A Swing County in a Swing State 35

PART 2: Stories of Principle

Chapter 3: The Poverty of Welfare and Its Destructive Effects
on Fatherhood 57

Chapter 4: The Unspoken American Genocide 71

Chapter 5: A Woman's Right to Defense 83

Chapter 6: Faith is Like Oxygen to Freedom 93

Chapter 7: Free Enterprise is to Compassion as Socialism
is to Oppression 105

Chapter 8: Lawfulness Leads to Peaceful Prosperity 117

Chapter 9: A Blue Hammer with a Red Heart 129

PART 3: A Critique of Modern Methods of Conservative Persuasion

Chapter 10: Persuading the Soul .145

Chapter 11: The Road Less Traveled 175

Acknowledgements 204

FOREWORD
by 2005 NFL MVP Shaun Alexander

The NFL MVP, All American Running Back, High School Football Player of the Year. All of these titles are how I am known nationally, but fewer know my backstory and my after-story.

Faith. Family. Freedom. These three pillars of America are also pillars in my life but not necessarily in that order.

Family. I was one of nine children fathered by my dad from four different women. My mother was a pillar of strength who emphasized faith in Christ as the answer. Her faith was unshakeable as she demonstrated that Jesus is always there when you have a need. Even though some days it was empty, whenever I went to open the refrigerator, I would see the quotation on the fridge "I know that I'm somebody because God doesn't make junk". I have learned that God can take brokenness and make it beautiful, including those whose lives have been wrecked by broken families. Today my wife and I have 11 children (yes, just the two of us!). Our family reflects the redemption that is possible for any American regardless of their background. There are more broken families now in America than ever before. This is sad because a unified family is one of the major keys to the success of our country.

Faith. My mom's teaching and modeling led to my decision to give my life to Christ at a young age. However, my faith became infectious once I grew to understand authentic discipleship while attending The University of Alabama. From that point forward, more than anything else, discipleship became the passion of my life. Throughout my football career I spent my time discipling and mentoring young men throughout the country to follow the ways of the Lord and to be driven by the Gospel of Jesus Christ. Many of these kids, some like me, coming from broken homes, were in dire need of a father-figure and mentor. I soon learned from the kids that I mentored that rules were not sufficient to prevent sinful behavior. They needed to have a vibrant relationship with Christ first and then integrity would follow. Many misunderstand the Gospel, they believe that religion is the way of faith. If America's youth are to awaken, it will not be through religious rituals or behavior modification, it will be through a vibrant relationship with Christ. The word faith can be interchanged with the words trust in or believe in. So, the question is, "does the next generation trust in, believe in, and have faith in Christ in every area of their life?"

Freedom. American culture has missed the mark when it comes to defining love. Culture defines love as a feeling, an emotion which compels us. This definition could not be farther from the truth. Love is defined by freedom because to love is to choose. When love is subject to the strength or weakness of one's emotions, it is no longer free. Love is a choice to have strong devotion and strong desires wrapped in truth. The choice to love one's children and spouse, one's neighbor, and one's community is demonstrated through fidelity and sacrifice when emotions run dry. Truth will enable you to find things about others that you didn't know. Love brings the freedom to be devoted to and to desire them even when something new is brought to light. This is the freedom most oft forgotten in America. Mankind is most free when his life is spent choosing to love. With freedom we can see things differently, still choose to love, learn each other's perspectives, and get under agreement. American freedom flourishes when its citizens choose to love.

Shortly after leaving the Seattle Seahawks to play for the Washington Redskins, I met Jon at a Christmas party in DC. Immediately,

I knew this was somebody who I was going to disciple. Our immediate bond led to countless hours of conversation, prayer, travel, and mentorship. The principles contained in this book are not just written words, they are truly authentic because they are lived by the author. How do I know this? I consider Jon as one of beloved spiritual sons, his words can be trusted because for more than a decade I've watched him live them out.

To those conservatives reading this book who want to change younger generations: the next generation of Americans is in desperate need of people who will make the choice to mentor, to sacrifice, to listen, to endure, and to invest in their lives when nobody else will. The object of this investment cannot be for political ends, they will see straight through the false pretense. Rather, choose a relationship demonstrated by devotion and desire wrapped in truth. The results of these kinds of relationships will allow millennials to see your life and will not only achieve a change in thought, it will result in the transformation of lives.

To millennials reading this book: regardless of your political convictions, I urge you to read with an open mind. This book will challenge you, inspire you, and motivate you to understand what you believe and why you believe it. Moreover, I believe that you will relate to pieces of these stories in more ways than you can imagine. The best things in life are worth seeking after, fighting for, and persevering through. I've taught others that you chase and attain what you really want, but you will find a way to let go of what you can take or leave. You have been offered a buffet of many claims but not much truth. Truth is not relative and not self-defined nor is it created by the emotions or passions of others. Let's seek truth. The journey for truth will require courage, so be courageous enough to pursue truth and you will find it. The ultimate goal is to understand who you are to God and then who you are to America.

—Shaun Alexander

PREFACE

Bellwether. The word elicits great excitement for Republicans and Democrats as applied to America's presidential election cycle. Its meaning is derived from the name given to the lead sheep of a domesticated flock; the leader would have a bell hung around its neck.[1] The word used in the American political context refers to states whose electoral outcomes decide the fate of the nation in presidential elections.

Lost in typical state-by-state analyses, however, are the thousands of smaller subdivisions (counties or their equivalents) that have powerful predictive voting behavior. Among these 3,142 subdivisions, 56 have been identified as bellwether counties since the year 2000 election cycle. One of those bellwether counties, Wood County, Ohio, happens to be the locus for the stories in this book.

Following the improbable results of the 2016 election, *Bellwether Blues* takes a deeper look into the bellwether county context to assess one specific demographic that appears to remain out of reach for conservatives: *millennial voters.* The de facto assumption is that education, worldview, and society render this generation as permanent fixtures of the Left. This book makes the bold claim that this assumption is untrue.

Wedged between an ideology that has abandoned them and an ideology they have been taught to hate, millennials appear to be stuck in a cycle of hopelessness, skepticism, and despair when considering the state of American political affairs. In other words, they have caught the *bellwether blues.* This book presents seven stories of millennials in bellwether-county America who were able to break this cycle.

To the conservative reader, the envisioned departure of many millennials from the Left is good news. But, surrounding this good news is the bad news that a departure from the Left does not necessarily mean an embrace of the alternative. Conservatives, who are often slower than progressives to adopt innovation, seem to have finally caught up technologically. But in the process, they have also been tempted to adopt the Left's tactics of political warfare.

The targeted reader is not the legislator, commentator, or figurehead, whose tactics of persuasion are intended to reach the masses. Rather, this message is for the conservative who remains out of the political spotlight. The strength of these individuals, who quietly go about their business, resides in the relational equity they have built over time. Adoption of the Left's no-holds-barred tactics in their relational networks would bankrupt these relationships, especially among millennials. Should this strategy of persuasion find a permanent home in the hearts of these patriots, conservatives will soon experience the *bellwether blues.*

The stories of this book will give these conservatives great hope, because each story proves that the greatest transformations of soul occur out of the spotlight. Each story, although unique, shares a common thread: the profound influence of others who invested in their lives. The stories show that the road to persuasion is the road less traveled. Persuasion requires sacrifice, selflessness, and the subsuming of a personal agenda. Often it means fewer people reached, but it also means a deeper reach into the life of a person. More than any previous generation, millennials are desperate for authentic relationships. In a culture measured by surface-level "likes," followers, and views, authentic face-to-face relationships carry immeasurably more value.

America is a nation built on the sacrifices of countless millions. In the words of Lincoln in his Gettysburg Address, "We can not dedicate, we can not consecrate—we can not hallow—this ground. The brave men, living and dead, who struggled here have consecrated it, far above our poor power to add or detract." Desperate to carry these sacrifices forward, my conservative friends ask, "What, then, can be done for my nation?" My counterintuitive proposition is to think deeper and to think smaller.

PART 1:

SETTING THE STAGE

CHAPTER 1:
The Millennial Dilemma

Once upon a time I was a liberal but liberalism has changed and I will no longer be a part of an ideology or a political party that represents everything that contradicts my values of unity, equal opportunity, personal empowerment, compassion, and love ... so I am walking away and I encourage all of you to [do] the same, #walkaway.
—Brandon Straka, The #WalkAway Campaign

Many conservatives, especially "seniors," have increasingly expressed alarm as they look toward the future, because of what they are witnessing in the present. Frequently, while I'm working in my office, one of my colleagues visits and shares his sincere concerns with me. Greg Rogers is a Marine from the baby boomer generation, Americans born between 1946 and 1964. Greg understands duty, sacrifice, and honor to the core. His perceptions are shared by the majority of conservatives of his generation, especially as they see the daily barrage of bias promoted by the mainstream media (MSM). As Greg said, "Walter Cronkite was a known Democrat, but as the most respected news anchor in America, he reported the news, not what he wanted people to *believe* about the news."

A widely held perception today is that the millennial generation will turn this nation as blue as the ocean. According to the MSM, younger generations are firmly entrenched on the left. To the MSM, this is great news. To Greg and his conservative generational peers, this is of significant concern. Often, Greg apologizes to me on behalf of millions of his peers—something like, "Jon, I have to apologize to you. I, and others of my generation, dropped the ball. I and we cannot help but be concerned as we think about the cultural and political change in America for our children and grandchildren, living in a nation where everything Americans most deeply cherish is being trampled asunder."

Greg's concerns are not unfounded. Federal and state education systems, the overwhelming bias of the MSM, and the draconian culture of corporate America hammer the Left's[2] agenda into the minds of millennials. The depressing conclusion for conservatives like Greg is that the millennial generation is destined to be a pawn of the leftist agenda. If Greg is right, America can expect a blue tsunami to change the political landscape of America, and soon.

The Democratic Party's concentration on leftist ideals in its platform throughout the 2016 and 2020 election cycles indicates the Left's confidence in this demographic tsunami. The 2016 Democratic Party platform reads like a Marxist tract. In interviews with random pedestrians in New York, documentary filmmaker Ami Horowitz of PragerU read excerpts from both the Democratic platform and *The Communist Manifesto*. The presumably left-leaning pedestrians struggled to distinguish the differences between the two platforms.[3] Such interviews could be conducted almost anywhere, and the results would be the same.

The philosophical divide between the Left and the Right has never been clearer. This chasm of separation between the two sides is the largest divide between political factions since the Civil War.[4] In an era where the policy positions of Democrats and Republicans stand in stark contrast, it is easier now than at any time in recent history for Americans to distinguish the differences between them. Consequently, it is easier to distinguish the outcomes of the two sides' policy positions and their impacts on society.

The stark contrast should make it easier for millennials to jump from one side to the other. But, what will millennials decide as they come to see the Left's and the Right's true colors? Will they stay with their home team, jump across the aisle, or ignore the whole controversy and not vote at all?

I'm afraid that in an age of skepticism, abandonment of political engagement is a legitimate possibility. As the data shows, millennials are likely to jump from left to center rather than from left to right. Unfortunately, the conservative approach to persuasion has grown increasingly pragmatic and short-sighted. As this book title notes, absent a change in conservative tactics, these voters are likely to experience the "bellwether blues," which will only increase their skepticism and decrease their trust in American political institutions. This result will induce conservative bellwether blues as conservatives become less represented by the people and therefore less represented in our institutions of government.

The bold contrast between Left and Right offers both sides a tremendous opportunity for political leaders to contend for the minds of people desperately seeking the truth. Arguments based on rage fill our social media outlets because they create the most immediate reaction. Social pressures, political correctness, and thoughtcrime limit the freedom of the millennial generation to question the status quo. Time and experience prove that arguments based on logic and fact will eventually find residence in the millennial mind. However, a jump to conservatism will require that its principles reach the soul. This is the long road, a road less traveled, but a road that will create the greatest and most lasting returns.

Before we get to tactics of persuasion (see Chapter 10), let's first investigate the root cause of this philosophical divide.

Leftism Defined

Much of this book focuses on the migration of millennials away from the Left. Were the Democratic Party's positions the same as they were in the 1980s, such a move would be unlikely. Why? Primarily because of the difference between *leftism* and *liberalism*.

Simply put, 21st-century *leftism* has turned sharply away from— to the left of—20th-century *liberalism*.

Many of the significant forces that have appropriated the term *liberal* in the 21st century are not, in fact, liberal, as defined by history. According to the Goodman Institute, "20th-century liberals continued to be influenced by the 19th-century liberalism's belief in and respect for civil liberties. In fact, as the last century progressed, liberal support for civil liberties grew and groups like the American Civil Liberties Union (ACLU) began to proudly claim the label 'civil libertarian.'"[5] Classical liberalism of the 19th century shared a foundation with Thomas Jefferson's political philosophy. It differed from 20th-century liberalism in its defense of economic liberties, but both were committed to civil liberties.

An example of the liberalism of the 20th century can be seen through the wide platform of Democrats in the 1990s, which welcomed disparate views and freedom for all. Varying coalitions within the Democrat Party of the late 20th century included representatives who were pro-life and pro-Second Amendment. Today, the idea of being pro-life and Democrat has all but been eliminated.[6]

Consider the Religious Freedom Restoration Act (RFRA) of 1993. Sponsored by Democrats with a nearly unanimous Senate vote, and then signed into law by President Bill Clinton, a Democrat, RFRA champions the rights of conscience for US citizens.[7]

Now consider two radically different illustrations of 20th-century liberalism versus 21st-century leftism.

Millennials are living in a time when the prevailing forces of culture have moved from a position of *liberalism* to *leftism*.

This transition has deserted many classical liberals who, while not considering themselves conservative, cannot embrace the radical transformation of the Democratic Party. Take, for example, Dave

Sharp Left Turn

20th-Century Liberalism	21st-Century Leftism
Tom is a baker. Tom is asked by a member of the KKK to bake a cake celebrating white supremacy. The liberals of the 20th century created organizations like the ACLU to protect Tom's First Amendment right of free speech to refuse to bake the cake.	*Tom is a baker. Tom is asked by a gay couple to bake a cake for their wedding. The Left of the 21st century seeks to punish Tom by forcefully shutting down his business, sending death threats, and defaming Tom.*

Rubin of *The Rubin Report*. A famous political talk show host and commentator, Rubin considers himself a classical liberal. Rubin says that the Left left him.[8] He criticizes modern progressives as "regressive," due to their hierarchy of oppression, which tyrannically suppresses free speech and freedom of religion.[9]

Classical liberal arguments founded on logic and reason have degenerated into purely emotional appeals based on identity politics. One perfect example of this change is reflected by then-President Obama's one-word criterion for a Supreme Court Justice: *empathy*.[10] Lack of empathy has become a rallying cry of the Left. A litany of evils defines lack of empathy: homophobia, Islamophobia, intolerance, racism, sexism, and xenophobia. A sociological term coined in the '80s has become the new buzzword to encapsulate these emotional appeals: *intersectionality*.

According to *The Oxford Handbook of Feminist Theory*, "Intersectionality is an analytic framework which attempts to identify how interlocking systems of power impact those who are most marginalized in society."[11] This buzzword, which has proliferated on the Left, ranks people by their minority status. The more "oppressed" your group, the higher your rank. At the top of the rankings are LGBTQ and racial minorities; at the bottom are white males and evangelical

Christians. This ranking system has created societal filters that monitor and suppress "hate speech" from the lower-ranking classes.

The battle of ideology that has taken root in America is largely a result of leftist tactics to monopolize political speech. Violence toward conservatives on campuses across America has revealed the logical results of suppression of speech. This tactic has already begun to alienate long-standing champions of liberty who traditionally voted Democratic, like Alan Dershowitz. Mr. Dershowitz is a famous constitutional and criminal law expert and a former Harvard Law School professor. Writing about the danger of leftism, he notes,

"Believing that noble ends justify ignoble means, they are willing to accept the antidemocratic, intolerant and sometimes violent censorship policies and actions of Antifa and its radical cohorts.... The danger posed by the extreme hard left is more about the future. Leaders of tomorrow are being educated today on campus. The tolerance for censorship and even violence to suppress dissenting voices may be a foretaste of things to come."[12]

The Left has appropriated the word *liberal* so effectively that now almost everyone—liberals, leftists, and conservatives—thinks *liberalism* and *leftism* are synonymous. But they're not.

In fact, liberalism and leftism have almost nothing in common. Here are six examples:

1. Race
Racial views are probably the most obvious difference between liberalism and leftism. The liberal position on race has always been a) no person should be judged by *the color of their skin*, they should be judged by *the content of their character*, and b) those who judge on the basis of race are racists themselves. Meanwhile, the Left believes the liberal attitude toward race is racist. That's why the University of

California officially identifies as racist the statement "There is only one race, the human race."[13]

Liberals have always been passionately committed to racial *integration*, while the Left is increasingly committed to racial *segregation*, such as all-black dormitories and separate black graduations at universities.[14]

2. Free Enterprise

Liberals have always been pro-free enterprise. They are committed to free enterprise, and they know capitalism is the only way to lift entire populations out of poverty.[15] Although it's true liberals want government to play a bigger role in the economy than conservatives do, they were never for socialism. The Left opposes capitalism and advocates socialism.

The success of the candidacy of Senator Bernie Sanders in the 2020 Democratic Primary is evidence of the Left's increasing influence. Throwing caution to the wind, many in the Democratic Primary have called for a full embrace of socialism in America.[16]

3. National Sovereignty

Liberals believe in the nation-state, whether that nation is the United States, Brazil, or France. But the Left opposes national borders, dividing the world by class rather than by national identity. So, while liberals have always wanted to protect American sovereignty and borders, the Left supports open borders.

When the writers of *Superman* were liberals, Superman was a proud American whose motto was "Truth, justice, and the American way." But that all changed a few years ago, when left-wing writers took over the comic strip and had Superman renounce his American citizenship to become a citizen of the world.

The Left has contempt for patriotism, seeing it as the road to fascism. They believe that we should all be "citizens of the world" in a world without borders.

4. View of America

Liberals have always venerated America. Watch American films from the 1930s through the 1950s and observe the overt patriotism produced, directed, and acted out by liberals. Liberals were aware of America's imperfections, but they still agreed with Abraham Lincolnthat America is "the last, best hope of earth." The Left, however, regards America as racist, sexist, homophobic, xenophobic, violent, and imperialistic.

5. Free speech

American liberals are known for being stalwart supporters of the famous maxim by Evelyn Beatrice Hall, "I disapprove of what you say, but I will defend to the death your right to say it."[17]

But the Left is leading the first widespread suppression of free speech in modern American history—from universities to tech companies to almost every other institution and place of work.[18] Of course, the Left claims to oppose only "hate speech." But the Left deems "hate speech" as anything that differs from their agenda. Any speech you or I consider hate speech but that the Left *agrees* with, however, is *free speech*.

6. Western civilization

Liberals have always championed and sought to protect Western civilization. Liberals celebrate the West's unique moral, philosophical, artistic, musical, and literary achievements, teaching them at universities around the country. The most revered liberal in American political history, President Franklin Roosevelt, often cited the need to protect Western civilization and even "Christian civilization." Yet, when President Donald Trump spoke of the need to protect Western civilization in a speech in Warsaw, the left-wing media, also known as the mainstream media, denounced him. They argued that Western civilization is no better than any other and that *Western civilization* is just a euphemism for *white supremacy*.

So, then, if liberalism and leftism are so different, why is the Democratic Party embracing the Left? There is no simple answer. The rise of Justice Democrats, the shift of major sources of money to the Far Left, the abandonment of independent journalism, and the long academic march toward leftism are all major contributing factors. But as one of the best-known liberals in America, retired Harvard Law School Professor Alan Dershowitz, said, "As a liberal, as an American, and as a Jew, I far more fear the Left than the Right."

Dear liberals: Conservatives are not your enemy. The Left is.

According to a Pew Research report entitled "The Partisan Divide on Political Values Grows Even Wider," the 21st-century shift toward extremes has happened much more among Democrats than Republicans.[19] Pew used a 10-item scale of political values to determine ideological purity among those who claim affiliation to one of the two major parties. Although both parties' lines have shifted, the data displays a titanic Democratic shift to the left of center during the 23 years between 1994 and 2017.[20]

The more the Left alienates the center, the more opposed leftism will become to traditional classical liberalism, challenging the

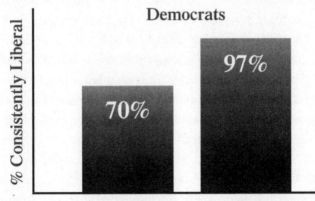

conservative once-secure position as liberalism's traditional foe. In other words, the Left's shift to the extreme left has the potential of making old-school liberals and conservatives allies.

What does this mean?

It means the day is coming when a whole subset of free-thinkers and defenders of liberty will rapidly vanish from the traditional Democrat voting bloc. This growing chasm separating the two major parties opens the gateway for a massive shift of millennials to move from the political left to the political right. Yet, absent a shift in conservative methods of persuasion, millennials are unlikely to cross the chasm to become conservative. Rather, they are more likely to become wandering political vagabonds. Skepticism will become their de facto political posture, and American institutions of government will suffer without the life-giving currency of trust with "We the People."

Size of the Millennial Demographic

Demographics prove that millennials matter. As of July 1, 2016, shortly before the 2016 election, millennials numbered 71 million, and baby boomers (ages 56 to 74 in 2020) numbered 74 million. Millennials overtook boomers in population in 2019 as their numbers swelled to 73 million and boomers declined to 72 million. Generation X (ages 40 to 55 in 2020) is projected to surpass the boomers in population by 2028.[21] The silent generation (ages 74+) will decrease to less than 20 million by 2028.[22] In other words, millennials will be the largest voting age demographic in America. Indeed, this is a generation with significant influence and the potential to shape the political landscape of our beloved nation. Thus, defining this generation is essential in a book investigating the convictions of this voting bloc.

How to Define a Millennial

The Pew Research Center, a self-proclaimed nonpartisan American fact tank based in Washington, DC, provides data on social issues, public opinion, and demographic trends shaping the United States and the world. Recently, Pew did a comparison of millennials with their grandparents from the silent generation. Here is the breakdown.[23]

Age Millennials were born between 1981 and 1996.[24] Thus, at the time of this writing in 2020, the millennials would consist of adults aged 24-39 years.

Education The heavy emphasis on education over the latter half of the 20th century seems to have made a difference, as today's millennials are much better educated than "silents" (members of the silent generation). Millennials will be the most educated generation in history by the time they complete their educational journeys. Millennial women are four times as likely as their grandmothers were to have at least a bachelor's degree at the same age. Nearly three out of 10 millennial men have at least a bachelor's degree, compared to 15% of their grandfathers when they were the same age.

Ethnicity Millennials are more likely to have descended from racial or ethnic minorities than are members of the silent generation. In 2017, fewer than 6 out of 10 millennials were non-Hispanic whites, compared with more than 8 out of 10 silents.

Marriage Millennials are more than three times likelier not to marry than silents were when they were the same age. Almost 6 in 10 millennials have not married, reflecting broader societal shifts toward marriage later in life.

Military Young silent men were 10 times more likely to be veterans than today's millennial men. Although millennials came of age at a time when the United States engaged in military conflicts in Iraq and Afghanistan after 9/11, they are far less likely to have served in the military than their boomer or silent predecessors.

Urbanization Larger shares of millennials today live in metropolitan areas than silent, boomers, and Gen X did when they were young. According to Pew Research Forum using data from 2017, "In 1965, when members of the silent generation were young, two-thirds lived in a metropolitan area, while one-third lived in non-metropolitan areas. And a similar share of baby boomers lived in metro areas when they were young. By comparison, more recent generations are residing in metropolitan areas at higher rates. More than eight-in-ten Gen Xers lived in metropolitan areas when they were young, and about nine-in-ten millennials today live in metro areas."[25] New research shows that this trend has become even more pronounced, as millennials are 21% more likely to purchase a home near a city center than Gen X.[26]

Women in the Workforce Millennial women today are much more likely to be working, compared to silent generation women during their young adult years. In 1965, when silent women were young, a majority (58%) did not participate in the labor force, and 40% were employed. Among millennials, that pattern has flipped. Today, 71% of millennial women are employed, while 26% are not in the labor force.

Millennial Political Breakdown Recent research from Pew also gave a breakdown of political leanings for the current American generations.[27] According to the research, millennial voters continue to have the highest proportion of independents of any generation. But when their partisan leanings are considered, they also are the most Democratic-leaning generation. More than 4 in 10 millennial registered voters (44%) describe themselves as independents, compared with 39% of Gen Xers and smaller proportions of boomers (32%) and silents (27%). However, a majority of millennials (59%) either affiliate with the Democratic Party (35%) or lean Democratic (24%). Just 32% identify as Republican or lean toward the GOP.

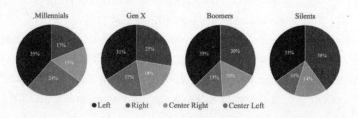

Pew's research buttresses this data with a survey showing a greater than two-to-one (62% to 29%) difference in millennial support for or leaning toward Democratic over Republican congressional candidates.[28] Based on this data, it would appear that the blue tsunami is on its way. As the electoral demographic shifts in the next two decades, is there any hope for the conservative movement?

Immediate Ramifications

Together, Generation X, millennials, and Generation Z now comprise a majority of voting-eligible adults in the United States, with millennials being the largest generation of the three.[29] But the size of a potential voting bloc means nothing if that bloc does not turn out to vote. Only when a *potential* voting bloc turns into an *active* voting bloc will it significantly influence elections.

Will the millennial bloc vote?

Millennials have demonstrated a lower voter turnout than any other generation.[30] Historically, younger adults are less likely than older adults to vote in midterm elections, and they have grown less likely with each generation.[31] Prior to the 2018 midterm elections, millennials had the opportunity to vote in four midterm elections (2002, 2006, 2010, and 2014). Among millennials who were ages 18 to 24 during these elections, 20% turned out to vote, on average. By comparison, 26% of boomers in that same age range turned out to vote in midterm elections between 1978 and 1986.[32]

However, 2018 represented a seismic shift in turnout. Millennial voter turnout for a midterm doubled from 20% to over 40%, increasing voter turnout to 26.1 million in '18 from 13.7 million in '14.[33] For the first time, Generation X, millennials, and Generation Z outnumbered baby boomers and the silent generation.[34] This data substantiates the importance of this generation as it decides the future of our republic. If millennials and subsequent generations decide to sustain their current voting patterns, the United States of America will take a radical turn toward the left.

Based on the data already presented, conservatives should pack their bags and go home. Is there any real hope to win the millennial generation?

A Millennial Split No, conservatives cannot win this entire generation. But, before you close the book with frustration, please carefully read this next sentence. Conservatives may not be able to win *the entire millennial generation* but they can win *a majority* of the millennial generation. And more specifically, they can persuade a certain type of millennial, who will only continue to grow in number as this generation grows in age. Thankfully for conservatives, the Left's departure from reality has opened the exit door to these individuals who pride themselves as being full of reason, reflection, and common sense.

Right when many millennials were entering the workforce, a 2013 *Time* magazine cover article pronounced the millennials as the "Me Me Me Generation."[35] As the world braced for this generation's entrance into the workforce, the millennial was guilty of narcissism before being proven innocent. Without a doubt, we all know people who fit the traditional stereotypes of millennials: lazy, entitled, dependent, selfish, woke, etc. Yet, as a millennial, the stereotype did not seem to apply to a majority of my millennial friends, whose lives were the exact opposite of the stereotype. I wondered if my network was the exception to the norm or if there was data to back up what I knew to be true.

Thankfully, I came across The Center for Generational Kinetics (CGK) and its founder, Jason Dorsey. CGK and its groundbreaking research validated my instincts: there is a major split among millennials. This split is defined not purely by age, race, gender, or civic engagement; rather, it is defined by *values*.[36] In fact, the group most offended by narcissistic, entitled, lazy millennials are *other* millennials who *do* defy these characteristics.[37] There is evidence that millennials delay "adulting" by a few years relative to previous generations, but according to the CGK, by the age of 30, they will self-select into one group or the other and can no longer relate to the other segment of their generation.[38] As Dorsey notes, these divergent trajectories will have profound implications for the workforce, marketplace, government, economy, and more.[39]

The group that self-selects into the non-stereotypical category is the group that conservatives can and must persuade. There are no guarantees for conservatives; a large majority of these *self-selectors* are already independent thinkers who prefer no party. Longitudinal research supports the move away from traditional party markers as more Americans in the early 2010s (vs. previous decades) identified as independent.[40] The good news for conservatives is that the independent streak of this generation, especially the "self-selectors," renders the current Pew Research data, the Left vs. Right snapshot, as highly elastic. The bad news is that all things held equal, traditional conservative tactics of persuasion are not working.

The Soul of the American Millennial

This book aims to explain why a majority of the millennial electorate will leave the Left based on life experience and principle. After meeting multiple millennials experiencing seismic shifts in their political leanings, a famous quote apocryphally attributed to Winston Churchill has often come to mind: "If you're not a liberal when you're 25, you have no heart. If you're not a conservative by the time you're 35, you have no brain."[41]

When speaking with the heroes featured later in this book, I found in each of them a deep conviction for truth. Each of these individuals was compelled to pursue the whole truth and nothing but the truth, because truth is precisely what our 21st-century world most lacks—and *craves*.

Wayne Gretzky, the undisputed greatest hockey player of all time, was once asked about the key to his success. Gretzky responded with resounding simplicity: "Skate to where the puck is going, not where it has been."[42] This simple statement has far-reaching application to our forecast of millennial voting patterns. The millennial bellwether blues result from frustration with what is viewed as a choice of lesser evils in our binary political system.

Leftism and conservatism, the polar-opposite philosophies high-lighted in this book, are represented within today's major political parties. Although parties do not embody the sum of the ideals of each philosophy, they are the life-giving apparatus. This fact frustrates many millennials. According to an NBC News/GenForward poll, 71% of millennials say that a third major party is needed.[43] Yet our winner-take-all political system leaves little chance for a third vehicle to break through the two-party barrier. The two dominant parties have a significant head start over third parties when it comes to national, state, and local infrastructure. Campaigns require cash, and cash requires confidence. Donors hesitate to donate to a small third party that may better represent their views but has little chance of winning at the ballot box.

US history confirms the two-party system is impenetrable, considering there has never been an extended period with three major parties. The Democrat Party, the oldest political party on earth, traces its roots back to the Democratic-Republican Party, founded by Thomas Jefferson and James Madison.[44] The Republican Party was formed in 1854 with the ultimate goal of abolishing slavery. Its rise to power was surprising, as other political parties rose and fell without significant success. It was founded on principle, as opposed to (and as a response to) the Whig Party, which had compromised on the issue of slavery. The Whigs were all but eliminated and replaced by the Republican Party after the primary election of Abraham Lincoln in 1860.[45] Over time, the two major parties have waxed and waned in power but have largely held death grips on their positions of power since 1860. Unless drastic change occurs, it can be safely predicted that the Democrats and Republicans will be the two entities vying for the votes of millennials during their lifetime.

Although the two parties are likely to remain in power, unsurprisingly, millennials have shown less fidelity to party than any previous generation. Millennials are less likely than older generations to vote "down the ticket" (meaning to vote for the candidates of only one party). A millennial's affiliation with a political party is comparable to a star high-school football player's verbal commitment to a college football team. It has limited meaning and changes on a whim.

Recent evidence points toward a thawing of Democratic Party passions among this demographic. A recent online survey performed by Reuters, a left-leaning international news agency, of more than 16,000 registered voters ages 18 to 34, shows their support for Democrats over Republicans for Congress slipped by about nine percentage points over the past two years, to 46% overall. And millennials increasingly say the Republican Party is a better steward of the economy.[46] While most millennials are likely to leave the Left silently, new movements like #WalkAway reveal seismic activity under the surface. Brandon Straka, a gay New York hairdresser, posted a video explaining why he is no longer a Democrat or a liberal. Within several weeks, the #WalkAway Campaign Facebook group attracted more than 172,000 members, and a multitude of WalkAway testimonies have been posted online.[47]

As the Left moves further to the left, the Democratic monopoly on the millennial generation is breaking apart. My experience as a millennial, and in speaking with others, is that deep in the soul of the American millennial exists a conviction to vote for principle over party or politician. Thus far, neither party has succeeded in securing the long-term allegiance of my generation's votes.

Whichever side captures the soul of millennials will also capture their voting allegiance.

CHAPTER 2:
A Swing County in a Swing State

Whoever wins Ohio … will win the presidency.
—*Albert R. Hunt, letter to the* New York Times, *October 2012*[48]

For the first time in my life, my political antennae were turned on when I moved to Washington, DC, shortly after Missy and I married in July 2008. This season of life could not have been more exciting, with the nation abuzz around the candidacy of a "once-in-a-generation" candidate, Barack Obama. My new colleagues at Georgetown were beside themselves as they considered the possibilities. Seemingly every conversation, every meeting, every event, was centered on this race.

Although I was in the tiny minority of voters in the greater DC area voting for the Republican presidential candidate, Senator John McCain of Arizona, it was impossible not to get caught up in the excitement. The two years that followed were only marginally less exciting, as the Obama administration launched its efforts to "fundamentally transform the United States of America."[49]

Thus, when my wife and I moved back to Ohio from Washington, we thought we were moving to a place of significantly less political importance and engagement. It might be an exaggeration to state that Wood County is a bastion of political engagement, but little did I know how important this county is to the DNA of what makes up America.

Every four years, America goes through the electoral exercise of determining a president. A presidential candidate needs to win 270 of a possible 538 electoral votes to win the presidency.[50] Many of the states, such as California and Texas, have been solidly blue or red, respectively, for decades. Regardless of the candidates, these states' votes had practically already been cast for one party before election day. Consequently, the outcome of the presidential election is determined by the handful of swing states, whose vacillating nature between red and blue awards them the label *swing*. By the numbers, presidential candidates spend most of their resources and time trying to woo voters from swing states. For example, 375 of the 399 presidential campaign events of 2016 were spent in swing states.[51]

Although there is some debate among political experts, most identify between 10 and 12 states as swing.[52] Among them, Ohio is the ultimate swing state. In the 38 elections dating back to 1860, Ohio has picked the winning president a staggering 34 times, including a streak of 14 elections dating back to 1960.[53] Ohio is only the seventh-largest state in terms of electoral votes, but its 18 electoral votes are pivotal, because they are the second-largest swath among the swing states (behind Florida, which has 29 electoral votes).[54] Win Ohio, and you have won the election.

Swing Counties: The Missing Key?

Often, the swing analysis stops at the state level. Yet states are large entities composed of millions of people. To get a more surgical grasp on the swing nature of a state, one must dig deeper. States comprise counties, the principal geographic and political subdivisions of each state. Apart from Alaska and Louisiana, where the equivalent units are called *boroughs* and *parishes*, respectively, every other state uses the term *county*.[55] Counties' principal functions include law enforcement, judicial administration, road construction and maintenance, the provision of public assistance to the needy, and the recording of legal documents.[56] Political parties follow this division of power, with autonomous national, state, and county party organizations.

There are 3,142 counties and county-equivalents in America.[57]

Only 59, or 1.88%, of those counties voted in the following pattern: Bush, Bush, Obama, Obama, Trump.[58] In the swing state of Ohio are 88 counties, and only three of them—Ottawa, Sandusky, and Wood— were among the 59.[59] Similar to the swing nature of the state, these counties have swung between parties in each election. Of note, several other larger Ohio counties (Hamilton, Lake, and Stark) have also demonstrated swing characteristics, albeit without getting each election "correct."

Surprisingly, the three Ohio counties that fit the analysis are exclusively located in northwest Ohio. Of the three, Wood County is ideal for examining millennial voter influence. Not only is Wood the largest in population and geography, but its population is also the youngest, with a median age of 34.7 years.[60] Thus, relative to the other Ohio swing counties, the vote's outcome will hinge on the decisions made by millennials.

I am not the first to recognize Wood County's unique proxy status. During presidential election years, Wood County attracts an overwhelming media presence, endless door-to-door campaigns, and countless pollsters. One memorable piece of media coverage is a 2012 presidential NPR *All Things Considered* segment on Wood County, entitled "Ohio County a Historic Predictor of State's Vote."[61]

Consequently, it is imperative to define what makes up Wood County and what makes it the pulse of the American voter. To answer these questions, I have consulted three main sources:

- the Citizens Financial Report created by the County Auditor for 2018[62]
- demographic profile data from the US Census Bureau[63]
- Data USA
- Understanding Wood County

History

Wood County was established on April 20, 1820, and is named after the 1812 war hero Colonel Eleazer Darby Wood, who led the construction efforts of the famed Fort Meigs in Perrysburg, Ohio.

Geography

Located in northwest Ohio, Wood County is directly south of Toledo. The county is the seventh-largest in the state, covering nearly 620 square miles.

Population centers

Wood County has 10 primary population centers, ranked here in order of 2018 registered voters: Bowling Green, 16,472; Perrysburg, 15,112; Perrysburg Township, 8,069; Lake Township, 6,875; Rossford, 4,193; Middleton Township, 3,450; Northwood, 3,054; Troy Township, 2,524; Montgomery Township, 2,275; North Baltimore, 1,851.[64] These 10 population centers represent 81% of Wood County registered voters as of July 2018.[65]

Population

At the time of the 2016 election, the population of Wood County was 130,492 and was 22nd of 88 counties in population size. Wood County has five cities, 21 villages, and 15 townships. Bowling Green is the largest subdivision, with 31,820 people.

Race

The population of Wood County is 88.8% White, 5.22% Hispanic, and 2.63% Black. Just 5.58% of the people in Wood County speak a non-English language, and 98.4% are US citizens.

Economy

The unemployment rate was 3.6% in March of 2019, which is 0.5% less than Ohio's unemployment rate. Total employment in the county was 67,500. Bowling Green State University was the largest employer, with more than 3,300 employees. In 2018, per capita personal income in the county was $45,163, and the median income for a family was $69,768.

The Perfect Proxy

Were it not for the heavy influence of the millennial vote, Wood County would likely be considered red. A majority of that influence has been consolidated at Bowling Green State University (my alma mater), where thousands of younger voters have swung the vote in past elections. However, the millennial vote in Wood County is shifting, especially as millennials deepen their roots within county lines.

Wood County's success economically and civically has spurred increasing numbers of young families to move into the county. This has grown the number of companies establishing roots within its jurisdiction. People have begun to take notice, as in 2018, Wood County was ranked one of the top ten Ohio counties to live in.[66]

On Wood County's northern border is Lucas County, home to Toledo, northwest Ohio's largest city. Every Lucas County office is held by a Democrat, and the county has been an entrenched Democratic stronghold for decades. In stark contrast to Wood County's growing population, Lucas has seen a steady *decrease* in population.[67] Due to Wood County's economic prosperity, safety, and generally thriving communities, many of its new residents are moving there from Lucas County.[68]

At this point, it is uncertain whether these new residents will bring their voting records with them, or whether they will adopt new voting patterns in a new setting. What is clear is that Wood County's population is getting younger. In 2012, its median age was 35.1, and in 2016 it was 34.7.[69]

Thus, Wood County's downward trend in age makes it the ideal proxy to gain a pulse on the millennial voter. As millennials grow older, establish roots, and have children, their voting habits are likely to change. The size of this shift is the variable that will determine the color of this swing county.

Millennial Voter Data from Wood County

It's no news that more voters turn out for presidential elections than for midterms and primaries. This effect seems to be accentuated in Wood County. Voters receive party status only if voting during a primary. Individuals voting only in general elections are identified as independents. Counties with younger voters are likely to have higher numbers of independents.

Registered independents hit a record-level 42% nationwide in 2018, 3% more than in 2016, and 5% more than in 2012.[70] True to their nature as swing voters in a swing county, 48% of all registered voters in Wood County were registered as independents in 2018.[71] Moreover, a closer look at the numbers reveals that millennials make up the bulk of registered independents in Wood County.

Overall Voters	R' Reg	D' Reg	I' Reg
Registered Party Votes	24869	16006	37551
total registered	78426	78426	78426
% of Registered voters	32%	20%	48%

18-39	R' Reg	D' Reg	I' Reg
Registered Party Votes	4550	4093	20445
total registered	29088	29088	29088
% of Registered voters	16%	14%	70%

40+	R' Reg	D' Reg	I' Reg
Registered Party Votes	20319	11913	17106
total registered	49338	49338	49338
% of Registered voters	41%	24%	35% [72]

As of 2018, 4,550 registered Republican voters and 4,093 registered Democrat voters were 18-39 years old. This means a staggering 70% of Wood County millennial voters are independents. A majority (55%) of the overall independent vote in Wood County is found in the younger population. This is the key swing vote that will determine the color of Wood County. The most strategic location in Wood County for the millennial vote is Bowling Green State University (BGSU).

Wood County Election Breakdown

Given the strength of the overall millennial vote, Wood County was expected to remain blue in the '16 election. To everyone's surprise, though, Wood County swung—and in dramatic fashion. Of Wood County's 97 voter precincts, Obama won 70% in '08 and 56% in '12. However, in '16, Trump won 73% of the precincts.[72] And, true to the proxy status of this county, the Wood County 8.6% differential closely reflected the state's 8.1% differential in favor of President Trump.[73]

2008 Overall	Obama	McCain
Total Votes	34285	29648
Vote Differential	4637	
%	54%	46%

2012 Overall	Obama	Romney
Total Votes	32802	29704
Vote Differential	3098	
%	52%	48%

2016 Overall	Clinton	Trump
Total Votes	27318	32498
Vote Differential	5180	
%	46%	54%

A close look at Wood County's map reveals four primary demographic factors, which reveal why Wood County is the ideal bellwether county.

1. Bowling Green State University (BGSU): With its student vote traditionally favoring Democrat candidates in vogue, BGSU makes this part of the county blue.

2. Perrysburg and Perrysburg Township: The northern-part of Wood County has the wealthiest population and is the fastest-growing. With a median age of 38, this thriving suburb of Toledo is a locus of young families. Traditionally, this population has voted red, but as the area has grown, it has attracted younger voters who have made it less so.

3. Rural Townships: Vast farmland stretches over much of Ohio's seventh-largest county. Townships and villages like Center, Freedom, Jackson, Jerry City, Middleton, Washington, and Webster represent a bastion of conservative values and voters. These are dark red.

4. Blue Collar Perimeter: Much of Wood County's border is filled with blue-collar workers. This population is filled with union labor and people who work in larger metropolitan areas: Toledo in the north and Findlay in the south. This demographic traditionally voted blue until '16.

Of the four demographics, two had the greatest impact on the '08, '12, and '16 elections: #1 and #4.

74

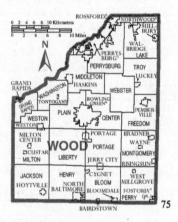

75

BGSU Students

BGSU is Wood County's largest employer and has more than 19,000 students enrolled at the main campus.[75] BGSU's student demographics are one reason for the high proportion of independent voters in the county. Voter registration drives that target younger populations are most common during the general election cycle. As already noted, anyone who doesn't vote in a primary while registered during a general election cycle is considered independent, regardless of his or her political affiliation.

Traditionally, Democrats and other interest groups from the Left have concentrated their registration efforts on BGSU's campus. Understanding the likelihood of capturing a vote in their favor, these groups establish an inescapable, overwhelming presence. Their success, or lack thereof, is part of determining the shade (if not the color) of Wood County during the election.

Logically, the data from Wood County should show not only a strong independent presence on campus but also a voting pattern favoring Democratic candidates. Let's look at the voter data from the precincts surrounding the campus of BGSU during the presidential years of 2008, 2012, and 2016.[76]

2008 Campus Precincts	Obama	McCain
Total Votes	4407	1726
Vote Differential	2681	
%	72%	28%

2012 Campus Precincts	Obama	Romney
Total Votes	4476	1660
Vote Differential	2816	
%	73%	27%

2016 Campus Precincts	Clinton	Trump
Total Votes	4110	1830
Vote Differential	2280	
%	69%	31%

The number of 18- to 39-year-old voters registered as Democrats in 2018 (4,093) was less than the campus vote alone for Democratic candidates in each of the past three general election cycles.[77] The high watermark for vote differential occurred in '12, in which Obama defeated Romney by 2,816 votes. Surprisingly, '12 also had more campus-voter turnout for Democrats than during the historic 2008 election cycle. Yet, countywide in '12, the enthusiasm for Obama was much more tempered than in '08. The rest of the county, sans BGSU, was just about even.

In 2012, the difference between the campus differential and the county differential was fewer than 300 votes. The BGSU vote carried the county for Obama in '12. Part of the success on campus resulted from concentrated registration efforts and Get Out the Vote (GOTV) activity. Golf carts loaded with pizza, snacks, and soda were transporting students by the dozens to their polling locations the day early voting began.

The big question in '16 was presumably whether BGSU could sustain the momentum of '12 to deliver the county to Hillary Clinton.

2016: The Year Everything Swung

Four years later, the tide changed, but not only on campus. In '16, no less of an effort was mobilized by the Democrats at BGSU. However, despite polling and public backlash to the Republican candidate, Donald J. Trump, their efforts fell flat. The BGSU campus differential shrank—from a 2,816-vote margin of victory for Obama in '12 to a 2,280-vote margin of victory for Clinton in '16. Fewer BGSU voters came out for the Democratic candidate, and more came out for the Republican candidate than in '08 and '12. Few pundits could have predicted such an outcome.

To make matters worse for the Democrats, in '16 the campus vote was no longer as influential to the overall countywide vote as in previous years. Clinton's 2,280-vote advantage from BGSU could not put a dent in the vote differential of President Trump from the rest of the county. What led to this differential? It was primarily Wood County's "Swing Precincts." A Swing Precinct in this analysis is a precinct with > 10% change in its vote from '12 to '16.[78] True to Wood County's bellwether status, in the '16 election, 53 of 97 precincts were designated as Swing Precincts. Incredibly, every single one of the 53 Swing Precincts swung in favor of Trump. This phenomenon led overall to an almost 8,000-vote swing from '08 and '12 to '16. Here are the numbers:

2008 Swing Precincts	Obama	McCain
Total Votes	17721	13833
Vote Differential	3888	
%	56%	44%

2012 Swing Precincts	Obama	Romney
Total Votes	17134	13264
Vote Differential	3870	
%	56%	44%

2016 Swing Precincts	Clinton	Trump
Total Votes	12169	16176
Vote Differential	4007	
%	43%	57%

Since BGSU students were not the major factor in the '16 election, who was? This is what leads us to the primary demographic that swung Wood County in 2016.

Wood County's Blue Wall

When considering the overall outcome, it was clear that Wood County reflected the sentiments of most people in Ohio. As the afternoon turned to evening on November 8, 2016, pundits would describe the impossibility of Trump winning in Michigan, Pennsylvania, and Wisconsin. These three states represented the "blue wall." It was unimaginable for a Republican candidate to win all three of those states. Nevertheless, Trump pulled off the impossible by scaling the "blue wall," winning all three.

Similarly, Wood County has traditionally held its own version of a blue wall along the northern border with Lucas County and the southern border with Hancock County. Had pundits looked at election results coming from the blue-wall precincts in Wood County, they likely would have predicted the outcomes in the blue-wall states. Let's take a closer look at three locations in Wood County filled with blue-collar, hard-working Americans. Traditionally these three locations have supplied Democrats a consistent vote in previous elections:

Lake Township, Northwood, and Rossford (my high school alma mater). Let's take a look at the numbers:[79]

2008 Blue Wall Precincts	Obama	McCain
Total Votes	7107	4651
Vote Differential	2456	
%	60%	40%

2012 Blue Wall Precincts	Obama	Romney
Total Votes	6814	4505
Vote Differential	2309	
%	60%	40%

2016 Blue Wall Precincts	Clinton	Trump
Total Votes	4976	5657
Vote Differential	681	
%	47%	53%

The reversal in Wood County's northern blue wall alone is a swing of more than 3,000 votes from the '08 and '12 elections. This region of Wood County has the prototypical characteristics of the working-class union vote, which became pro-Trump in '16. Within the Wood County northern blue wall precincts, the median household income is $56,806, and the median age is 40.9.[80]

As seen from this brief comparative election analysis, while student voting represents a major bloc, the county's population growth increasingly dilutes the power of this voting bloc. Voter turnout is increasing in growing Wood County communities like Bowling Green, Lake Township, Rossford, Perrysburg, and Perrysburg Township. Absent unusual enrollment numbers at BGSU, Wood County population growth will give increasing importance to the rest of the county in every subsequent election.

Looking ahead to the ever-consequential 2020 election and future elections, millennials, now in the workforce and raising families, will make up a growing proportion of Wood County voters. As a bellwether of bellwethers, Wood County millennials merit a closer look.

Why? Because whoever wins Wood County wins Ohio, and whoever wins Ohio wins the presidency. To the party most successful at wooing this voting bloc belongs the coveted electoral prize. As I will further explain, the winning party will be the one who awakens the millennial soul.

PART 2:

STORIES OF PRINCIPLE

Man is still the greatest miracle and the greatest problem on this earth.
—David Sarnoff

People travel to wonder at the height of the mountains, at the huge waves of the seas, at the long course of the rivers, at the vast compass of the ocean, at the circular motion of the stars, and yet they pass by themselves without wondering.
—St. Augustine

As the earlier chapters have explained, the millennial generation is beginning to abandon the Left, but the 270-electoral-vote question is "Why?" According to T.D. Jakes, the famed black minister, "There is nothing more powerful than a changed mind." And the best way to demonstrate that is through storytelling. So, rather than look for answers from poll data or from third-party sources, I went to the source, "We the People."

I limited my audience by using four qualifiers:

1) US citizen
2) Current Wood County resident [81]
3) Supported Obama in '08 or '12 and Trump in '16 [82]
4) Millennial as defined by Pew Research Center (see Chapter 1)

None of the interviewed individuals are rich or famous. But, in this book, I refer to them as the everyday heroes who advance the timeless vision of our Founders. Frankly, I admire their courage to allow their stories to be told publicly, come what may.

The more I got to know our seven heroes, the more encouraging my outlook on America became. Many suppose Alexis de Tocqueville to have said, "America is great because she is good, and if America ever ceases to be good, she will cease to be great."[83] This book's interviewees are the good people who make our nation great. Their stories should give hope to the despairing conservatives of the silent generation and inspire the younger generation of millennial conservatives.

Not Who You Think

The '16 election has been thoroughly analyzed. Much of the analysis has classified the Trump voter as a working-class voter who generally thinks life is getting worse. The book *Hillbilly Elegy* gives context to this story by looking at lower- and middle-class whites in the Appalachia region.[84] Recent books such as *Coming Apart* and *Bowling Alone* have doubled down on the claims of the *Hillbilly Elegy*. Indeed, the scaling of the "blue wall" in Michigan, Pennsylvania, and Wisconsin would not have been possible without this vote.

Yet, as my investigation has shown, a Trump victory in '16 would have been impossible without a much broader coalition. Indeed, elections in '20 and beyond will also require a broad coalition. My investigation seeks to fill a gap in the mainstream analysis by identifying voters who are not typical, according to other literature. Their stories are powerful. Their backgrounds are diverse. Many of these stories defy the logic of intersectionality, being made up of minorities and women whose life experiences drove them away from the political Left to the political Right.

Whether these voters will continue to vote for Trump is unknown, but undoubtedly there are principles that inform their decision-making. Each of them was won over through life experience, wise mentors, and by the stories of others, who were hurt by the Left's agenda. Concerned for the welfare of their fellow citizens, these individuals decided change was necessary.

Because conservatives too often struggle to persuade the heart, they have traditionally struggled to win voters like the seven in this book. Logic can go only so far to influence people's decisions. Millennials supposedly weigh emotion and logic equally in decision-making. But as Chapter 10 reveals, emotions play a much larger role in the framework of human decision-making than anticipated. Even postmodern architecture reflects this pattern, as buildings are being constructed to reflect the way people feel.[85] Emotional intelligence (EI, or EQ) has climbed the ladder to become a buzzword in modern leadership literature. Those who can connect with others' feelings will thrive.

Emotional intelligence is a series of competencies leaders use to recognize emotions—theirs and other people's—to discern different feelings. Having labeled feelings appropriately, leaders use this information to guide others' thinking and behavior to achieve their goals.[86]

According to a Levo Institute survey, 80% of millennials strongly believe that cultivating emotional intelligence is key to career development.[87] Companies that value the emotions and feelings of employees are expected to retain the lion's share of millennial talent.[88]

Millennials value emotional intelligence in and out of the workplace and certainly in the world of politics. Beto O'Rourke, although a privileged upper-middle-class white male (according to the Left's intersectionality logic), became the Left's star of the '18 midterms. More than $70 million poured in from all over the country to help O'Rourke try (unsuccessfully) to unseat Senator Ted Cruz.[89] The embrace of O'Rourke as a star was largely due to his unique ability to capture emotions and persuade through storytelling. By explaining his far-reaching leftist policy positions with story and charisma, Beto brought his leftist views closer to the voter.

The stories of the heroes interviewed for this book teem with experiences, emotions, and facts that changed the way they look at life.

As we transition from '16 to '20 and beyond, one thing is clear: Facts alone will not suffice. Conservatives must use *story* to explain the facts and persuade the voter. Then, and only then, will a majority of millennials be won to the right side of the political table.

Before delving into the stories of the true heroes of this book, here is my awakening story, which ultimately led to the writing of this book.

My Story

I am a millennial—barely, depending upon how that is defined (see Chapter 1)—born in October 1982, into a middle-income family of six children in Toledo, Ohio. When my dad left his career to become a pastor, our income level was such that we qualified for paid school lunches. Although we were not wealthy by American standards, in global terms, I hit the jackpot: I was born in America and had loving parents who taught the Bible.

Wealthy or not, each household in America is part of civil society. So, like everyone else's, my political journey began at home. Yet, all was quiet on the political front until my mid-20s.

One day in 2007, as I sat at my desk in Houston working for a publicly traded company, an article flashed across my computer screen that would change the trajectory of my life. The article highlighted the leadership of former Democratic congressman and ambassador Tony Hall in the American political world on the issue of global food security. Immediately, I came alive. Something resonated within me that heightened a stark contrast between Mr. Hall's lifework and the path I had chosen.

This moment led me to a crossroads. The more I thought about the article, the more I knew I needed to change. At that time, my fiancée (now wife of 10+ years) was living in DC, and our post-wedding plans were to live in Houston. She immediately reached out to a couple of people to ask about Mr. Hall. Miraculously, her landlord informed her that he lived on the same block. Neither of us could believe it.

The serendipitous series of events led us to pursue a life in DC. One month later, after taking a test for graduate school, I was accepted into Georgetown University's Public Policy Institute (GPPI). Six months after that, Missy and I were married, and graduate school began in the fall of 2008. I was newly married, active in a vibrant church, launching a nonprofit, and attending Georgetown while Missy worked as an event planner. Everything was working out well beyond my expectations. I was destined to become the next Tony Hall in two years … or so I thought.

Not only did I get to meet Mr. Hall (briefly), I was offered the opportunity to interview to become his assistant.

Then, to everyone's surprise, I turned the interview down.

I was convinced that if I were going to make an impact, I would need to fulfill my commitment to graduate school at Georgetown.

To this day, I hold the highest regard for many of my GPPI colleagues. They were kind, bright, driven, and full of conviction. Yet their political convictions were as diametrically opposed to my political traditions as could be. It was the fall of 2008, and I was surrounded by these bright, liberal young leaders, who were convinced Barack Obama was better than sliced bread. I quickly learned I was in a minority of students who were willing to vocalize their support for John McCain and Sarah Palin.

Much to my chagrin, my leftist colleagues were persuasive in their philosophical arguments in support of then-candidate Barack Obama. To their credit, they would patiently listen to my surface-level defense of the Republican nominees, only then to destroy my points with valid reasoning filled with conviction. I felt like a leaf in the wind. The more I grasped at reason, the more I knew that I was undone. I was no match.

This disconcerted me. According to Gallup's Strengthfinders (now CliftonStrengths), one of my top five strengths is Belief. For much of my life, I had devoted my research to topics like the origin of the universe and the life, death, and resurrection of Jesus Christ. I could debate with almost anybody on matters of faith. I knew what I believed and why.

But in the debate of political values and philosophies, a battle had begun in my mind. Over the next two years, I was at a stalemate. I heard logical arguments from my colleagues, but none that could entirely shake me from those homegrown values that informed my political leanings. Many tried to recruit me into the Democratic Party, and I entertained making the leap. However, as with my faith, I wanted to make sure to base my political conclusions on thoughtful research and truth. I needed to go deeper.

An opportunity to dive deep presented itself shortly after Missy and I returned from graduate school to northwest Ohio. Once again, to the surprise of many, we declined opportunities to stay in DC, deciding instead to return to Ohio to launch a business committed to helping raise people out of poverty. The busyness of graduate school was replaced with a global job leading to international flights and large blocks of time to read, meditate, and debate with friends and mentors. More importantly, my life was filled with my first child, a beautiful daughter named Emelia.

The convergence of these events presented the desperately needed perspective to weigh the arguments presented by the Left and the Right, not necessarily for my own benefit, but now for the benefit of raising my child. Throughout my international travels, my appreciation for American citizenship only grew. I developed a fascination with our history, our politics, and our way of life. I developed a voracious hunger for American history. The more I read, the more my convictions crystallized. In my soul an awakening took place that led to a wholehearted embrace of the Party of Lincoln.

This book is a compilation of stories of people who, although they differ from me in appearance, are similar to me in soul. These are Americans who began their journey following the status quo of liberal progressivism. However, like me, these individuals were persuaded by principles that reached their soul, which then led to a transformation of mind.

Many of the millennials interviewed for this book traveled farther and harder than I did to reach their "awakening." Some have been opposed by family and friends. All have demonstrated immense courage of conviction.

I believe that by reading their stories and by learning about the convictions of like-minded Americans, you will be better equipped to stand for truth in the hour when our nation most needs it.

CHAPTER 3:
The Poverty of Welfare and Its Destructive Effects on Fatherhood

PREFACE

No greater crisis faces our nation than that of the fatherhood crisis. With 1 out of 4 children living in a home without a father, broken homes pervade our nation.[90] This problem has particularly become an epidemic in inner cities.[91] The trend has been steady for more than seven decades, and the central question is "Why?" In research by the National Health Statistics Report, among the variables that most influence positive outcomes for children, two relate directly to the father: fathers living with their children, and the marital status of the father.[92] These variables raise greater questions that were not asked in the report, including what role, if any, welfare plays in destabilizing nuclear family structures. In the book *The Poverty of Welfare,* by Michael Tanner of the Cato Institute, the author makes the case that there is a significant correlation between welfare dependency and the dissolution of the father's involvement in the family unit. Practically speaking, welfare penalizes married couples, creating perverse economic incentives for women to have children out of wedlock.

In an astounding statistical paradox to modern-day expectations, Tanner notes that the most insured demographic in the early 20th century were African-American households.[93] In the face of overwhelming racism that eliminated black families from government benefits, it was the fraternal organizations, churches, and businesses of the black communities that stepped forward to provide support for orphans and widows in the community. Single, able-bodied, young black males and females were not eligible for such support; they were required to get a job. Families were financially stronger together rather than separated. These fraternal organizations disappeared from their once-influential role, as the governing entities increased in their influence and presence in black communities. According to Tanner, the loss of influence of local fraternal organizations has reduced the ability of black communities and local leaders to solve local problems.

THE STORY OF **ARRON LAWRENCE**

Originally from Cleveland, Ohio, Arron Lawrence, a black millennial, decided to raise his family in Bowling Green. Arron grew up with both of his biological parents. His family was a family of faith, attending church regularly. His dad would read the Bible, but they did not pray and read the Bible together as a family, as Arron would later resolve to do with his children. It was not until his mom got sick with breast cancer that they prayed as a family. His mom recovered, but she then got leukemia and died his freshman year of college in 2007. Arron had prepared for this and spent as many precious moments with her as possible. Those years built lifelong memories that would empower Arron to live a life to honor his mom. Knowing what his mom required of him enabled Arron to become an overcomer, which is the moral of his story.

As Arron grew up in inner-city Cleveland, his mom was a mother to everyone. She was someone you could trust and rely on for comfort. She always saw the good in everyone and was an incredible woman. Arron's dad was a great dad, present in the home and in his sons' lives. Of his friends, Arron was the only one with a dad in the home.

Arron's family was a strong, solid, working-class family. Before she died, Arron's mom worked at his school, and his dad worked nights at the Cleveland Clinic. His dad helped get his sons to school in the morning, and he attended all of Arron's extracurricular events. From a young age and through his high school years, Arron knew his dad's presence was significant. Arron's parents worked to ensure that their children would not experience the poverty of welfare, and they worked to give them the best education possible. Thus, Arron had the advantage of attending a private Catholic school. His school comprised mostly black students from homes with both parents present, in stark contrast to the homes of his neighborhood friends.

Church was a major influence in Arron's upbringing; he participated in Cub Scouts, Bible studies, and Sunday school. Once Arron went to high school, he didn't want to be in the choir anymore, so he joined the junior deacons club, which conducted devotions before the ministers would come out to start the service. Arron had some great mentors in this organization who emphasized faith and education. Nevertheless, many of Arron's junior deacon peers, himself included, treated faith more as a formality than as a foundation for all of life. The hearts of many of the kids, Arron included, were not into the program. They participated only because they were forced to by their parents or guardians. It would take time before the lessons of faith from these early years would find residence in Arron's heart.

In middle school, sensing Arron's strength of character, his parents decided to send him to the local public school. Arron's appreciation for his dad only grew as he again found himself in a small minority of students who had a dad involved in their lives. Although there was not much violence at his public school, violence pervaded his neighborhood. Drug dealers, gang members, and other ill-actors roamed constantly. Police chases, shootings, and fights were routine in Arron's neighborhood. Having a strong nuclear family helped Arron say no to the wrong choices. Thankfully, for Arron and his friends, other strong local black male leaders took up the charge to empower the next generation. One gentleman gave black youth an opportunity to see life beyond Cleveland through a mentorship program.

In addition to his parents and other community leaders, Arron's brother, 14 years older, eventually proved to be a role model. His brother had played football at Ohio Northern University but did not finish his studies there, so he came home and began working toward an associate's degree in architecture. Arron's brother then accepted Christ and participated in ministry, which moved him to Arizona. At that point, he began to exercise his faith.

Prior to this transformation, Arron's brother had associated faith only with church on Sunday. His influences had come mainly from rap artists like Puff Daddy and Tupac. These influences led him to partying, drinking, smoking, doing drugs, and womanizing. Upon returning home, it was a moment at church that led him to the light. He knew he needed to make a change, and change he did.

Meanwhile, church was waning as an influence in Arron's life. Arron's transformed brother stepped in just in time. While Arron was in middle school, he helped Arron make right decisions, warning him of pitfalls he had fallen into years earlier. Arron looked up to his brother (and still does), and it was this engagement that helped cement Arron's convictions.

Political Leanings

According to Arron, his family had always voted exclusively as Democrats, but the Lawrence family's values were much more conservative than they were liberal. But not once did they meet a Republican who could make a principled case. In fact, Arron does not recall even meeting a Republican while growing up. It was the Lawrence family's foregone conclusion that the Democratic candidates alone supported political issues that directly impacted black citizens.

Two major issues were prioritized in Arron's community: welfare and criminal justice. The community's most vocal members were the political leaders and the community organizers whose interest primarily resided in acquiring power by delivering benefits to the community. Thus, any attempt to reduce these benefits in any way was viewed as a racist sentiment. Another major issue that entrenched the black vote in favor of Democrats was the issue of incarceration. Because virtually every family in the community was affected by the criminal justice system, many looked for an empathetic voice, but also one that could deliver security. The stigma attached to Republicans was that they abandoned people with criminal records.

Arron's parents limited their political engagements to voter registration and to handing out literature for family friends running for local political offices. Although both voted for Democrats, Arron's dad was more engaged than his mom in political activities. Nevertheless, little about politics was mentioned in the Lawrence household. No expectation was placed on Arron regarding how he should vote. However, one thing consistently preached in the Lawrence home was their opposition to welfare as it existed. To Arron's dad, the Democratic politicians had this wrong, and this would make a deep impression on Arron's voting future.

The Poverty of Welfare

According to Arron's dad, welfare is overwhelmingly used as an excuse by its recipients to avoid work and can destroy someone's will to live a life of virtue. As Arron grew, the more he witnessed welfare's destructive effects. Many of the welfare recipients Arron knew leveraged welfare benefits while diving headfirst into a life of crime, with money coming from black-market activities. Arron saw many single young ladies turn from students to dropouts as welfare dependents. Many of those young ladies were second-generation welfare dependents, getting pregnant out of wedlock at an early age. Arron could not help but witness a devastating trend as these once-ambitious young ladies unnecessarily settled for dependence on the system. Welfare further decreased the likelihood of a woman getting married. Marriage seemed unnecessary if they could glean their own financial stability on their own. This logic would turn into a vicious cycle with live-in boyfriends and broken homes with multiple children from multiple fathers.

Nevertheless, Arron's dad pointed the blame at the fathers. Most of the boyfriends of these women would abandon their partner and children. Often, these young fathers would instead choose a life of crime. He believed that if fathers would become *dads* who provide for their families, there would be no need for welfare. Arron's dad believed that by embracing the principles of Christianity, a father would do everything within his power to avoid welfare for his children.

The issue hit close to home: Arron had some extended family members who were dependent on welfare. Joining welfare impacted the status of that family member and his or her children. Arron's family and community looked down on welfare. Welfare coupons generated a stigma in society. Someone with welfare coupons was seen as being in a lower, less-accomplished class. Arron was not allowed to spend significant time with kids from homes that received welfare, because his parents were concerned about their influence in his life. They observed that a lack of rules and structure surrounding these children led to perverse behavior patterns.

Among the generation of the children of welfare recipients, Arron noticed a culture of lawlessness. Young ladies especially would fail to live out their destiny, because they did not have a father's affirmation. According to Arron, when you don't know your value and worth, you will fall for anything. Absent a father, many of these ladies would be taken advantage of, looking for love in all the wrong places. He also noted that the expectation of welfare families was to fall in line with the generational cycle of dependency. Any attempt to rise above this culture would be criticized and condemned. The expectation was for these young ladies to become young mothers as welfare dependents. From Arron's perspective, expectations often became reality as their culture and path toward survival merged. A tidal wave forced them in the opposite direction of independence.

Welfare's rules eliminated any incentive for families to generate lawfully gained income through work. Increasing their legitimate income would disqualify families from receiving welfare funds. So, many welfare families enlisted their children to steal, cheat, and sell drugs to supplement welfare benefits. Arron believes welfare promoted these families' bad choices. Absent welfare, the mothers would be less likely to have multiple partners. Instead of petitioning the state for resources, they would look for better, stable, and faithful men, who would provide for their children. This would lead to increased fidelity and stability in the home for the children.

Arron also recognized that to break the cycle of welfare dependency, men would need to become more responsible. The state should not subsidize deadbeat fathers who are unemployed, vagrant, and reckless. For these fathers, eligibility for government benefits should depend upon their faithfulness to their children and to those children's mothers.

Arron saw welfare as damaging to the family structure.

The 2008 Election

Arron studied at BGSU from fall 2006 through fall 2011. He noticed the culture shock among his black friends as they met white students. But Arron's dad, having already set the tone for the Lawrence household, encouraged Arron to embrace diversity and treat others equally, regardless of race.

Even while most of Arron's worldview was changing, his political perspective remained largely unchanged. During the fall of 2008, BGSU's campus was abuzz with excitement for Barack Obama. Everybody was excited to be a part of history, to participate in the change he was promising. Many students put all their hope in this presidential candidate. Arron doubted such hope was warranted. He believed that the most important questions in life could be resolved only by God.

But his skepticism did not dissuade him from casting a ballot in favor of Barack Obama.

Back home, Arron's dad encouraged him to vote but never discussed the candidates. The unspoken expectation among Arron's community, however, was that, as a black man, he would vote to support the first black president. According to Arron, without question, the number-one reason black people voted for Obama was that he was black. Arron's vote in 2008 would be no different.

BGSU and Music

Election aside, Arron's new collegiate community grew more diverse. Arron's natural state was to keep to himself, but he was always open and congenial, hanging out with anyone and everyone who so desired. He became involved in a few campus organizations, including Sport Management Alliance, Fellowship of Christian Athletes, Black Student Union, and Impact. Of those, Impact was by far the most influential; he committed his life to Christ through Impact and found the greatest unity in diversity. Impact had an incredible mixture of races, and it is where Arron first saw faith lived out with authenticity. Everything from jail ministry to Bible studies to outreach shaped Arron's perspective and personality.

In 2009, when Arron joined Impact, he began to comprehensively assess the impact of issues on society. Whether life, marriage, economics, or race relations, Arron began to consider these through the lens of Scripture. For the first time, Arron understood the relevance of his faith to everything that he did, and it changed him to the core. For example, one of the major issues that shifted in his life was the recognition of secular music as poisonous to his mentality. The testimonies of other students he respected, who had eliminated from their lives music centered on sex, drugs, and violence, resonated with Arron. He desired a transformation of heart and mind. Once Arron replaced secular music with gospel music, a chain reaction ensued, and Arron began to experience change in other areas of his life.[94] Arron began to be transformed by the renewing of his mind; he became a new person from the inside out, and the way he viewed the world changed.[95] Perhaps most significantly, this transformation would shape one of the most significant decisions he would ever make.

Marriage and Life Post-BGSU

Two weeks after turning 21 years old, Arron, who thought he'd be excited about drinking, was thinking about something else: *marriage*. Arron met Chalese through a mutual friend prior to his wholesale transformation in the spring of 2007. Chalese, from Detroit, was a natural complement to Arron's personality. It wasn't long before they grew in affection and became an "item" the following semester. The relationship progressed rapidly and, like most other college couples at BGSU, they began to consider moving in together. The convenience of this decision, however, was interrupted by a crisis of conscience. Both Arron and Chalese began to question the move-in as they grew in faith at Impact. They decided to seek counsel from family members and pastors, who encouraged them to wait. In addition to biblical reasoning, the counselors surprisingly used statistics, which showed that living together before marriage would decrease the probability of a successful marriage.

The advice worked, but not in the way most would anticipate. Arron and Chalese decided they would move in together after all, but only after they got married immediately. To everyone's surprise, they eloped at a local courthouse without fanfare. This came as a shock to Chalese's family especially. Naturally, many voices critiqued this seemingly abrupt decision. Her parents felt they were too young, too immature, and too blinded by young love to see the truth. However, it was the voices of the young couple's friends of faith and of some of their closest family members who would win the day. From these stakeholders, Arron and Chalese would receive overwhelming support both immediately and for the rest of their marriage.

In the fall of 2009, they tied the knot. Arron and Chalese had been dating for two years before they married. Admittedly, Arron still had a lot of growing up to do, but he says marriage was one of the best decisions of his life. Undoubtedly, it was also a life-changing decision, with many mountains to climb and storms to weather. Their marriage flourished during the first year, but an event was coming that would test everything in his life, his marriage included. Similar to many other students graduating into a sluggish economy, Arron struggled to find a job. Being one of a handful of college graduates from his extended family, Arron had always thought landing a job was all but guaranteed. Arron did not invest significant time in the job search process; as a result, nothing came through. For the next year, Arron remained jobless. Tension began to grow in his marriage. His self-esteem took a major hit. For the first time in his life, Arron would have to seek temporary government support to weather the storm. This crisis escalated when the couple learned that Chalese was expecting a baby. Arron knew he needed a job to put food on the table.

Their family was growing—and fast. Not only were they pregnant with their firstborn, Chakir, but they were also looking into adopting Chalese's nephew, Cor'Neal. Cor'Neal was born in Detroit, Michigan. His mother died in a car accident when he was six months old, and his father died when he was three; a ceiling had collapsed on him. These tragic events led the Lawrences to bring Cor'Neal into their home. Without immediate intervention, Cor'Neal could have fallen into the issues faced by young black boys without fathers. Jobless or not, Arron and Chalese would not let this young boy become another statistic. They welcomed Cor'Neal into their home around the same time they welcomed Chakir into the world.

Now with four mouths to feed, Arron and Chalese grew desperate. For the first time, they began to question not only their marriage but also the foundation of their faith. Conflict and disillusionment began to shake them. Financial problems, often cited as one of the primary reasons for divorce, began pushing this couple to the edge.[96] In the midst of this challenging season, Arron was going to see if the president would make good on his promises of hope and change.

The 2012 Election

As the 2012 election drew near, Arron's personal financial crisis influenced his perspective on the election. Arron grew disillusioned by President Obama's positions on gay marriage, abortion, and economics. The lack of change that occurred in the communities who had placed their hope in this president frustrated Arron. For the many promises made, Arron saw very few being delivered. He saw only increased dependency, entitlement, and conflict.

Besides Obama's personality and likeability, nothing stood out that would help Arron support the president. At the same time, Mitt Romney did not seem like someone who sincerely cared about change for the country. For Arron, he seemed like a wealthy, out-of-touch politician who was not relatable to citizens like Arron, making it impossible for Arron to vote for the Republican candidate. At the same time, his disillusionment with Obama's failed promises caused Arron to sit on the sidelines in 2012.

Arron's "no vote" reflected a seismic shift in his heart. The "once-in-a-generation" candidate of Barack Obama, the first black president, the hope of the people, was no longer getting a pass from Arron because they were both black. Yet, Arron saw no viable alternative on the 2012 ballot.

During Arron's crisis, neither the skin color nor the wealth of people he knew determined his survival. It was a diverse community of faith, who were driven by deeper principles.

Consequently, what mattered to Arron was that the candidate he voted for be principled, honest, and personable. Neither Barack Obama nor Mitt Romney measured up.

Post-2012 and -2016

As the 2012 election came and went, the Lawrences were barely scraping by. Arron could not stand the thought of becoming welfare-dependent and knew a change was necessary to avoid this deadly trap. He was desperate for a breakthrough. Their marriage hanging in the balance, Arron recognized that the people who cared most about him and his marriage were his friends of faith.

A breakthrough occurred when Arron and Chalese reached out to their faith community for support. Immediately, people of faith from their college years and their church stepped in to assist. In addition to prayer and counseling, these friends helped Arron become employable. From his resume to his appearance to his pitch, they helped turn Arron into a professional interviewee. Arron's mindset began to change as he grew in confidence and resolve.

Eventually, Arron scored a stable, low-paying job. For most college grads, this job would seem reprehensible, but for Arron, it was a saving grace. He knew that being faithful in low-paying jobs would prepare him for higher-paying ones. This first job was at Rent-A-Center, and it was his first step outside of the financial storm.

Once Arron got a job, his marriage began to recover. But the wounds from this season were deep and would take long to heal. No longer qualifying for government assistance, the Lawrences were living on a razor-thin budget, which continued to bring stress into the home. Unable to afford some of the things other families enjoyed, Arron and Chalese had the choice to grow in bitterness or to grow in gratitude. Thankfully, they chose the latter.

Arron's faithfulness in his low-paying job paid off. Within a year of scoring his first job, Arron gained full-time employment with Enterprise Rent-A-Car. The financial relief was huge for their marriage. This job could not have come at a better moment, as Chalese was now expecting again.

Throughout the next four years, the Lawrence family would move from the poverty line to just above it, and then into the middle class. The stresses of their financial crisis could have broken this family, but instead, the family grew stronger. Arron credits his community of faith. Absent this community, the Lawrence family could have easily become another statistic. Instead, the Lawrence family modeled faithfulness and generosity. Recognizing the measure of grace and love they had been given, they became a model of the same to others.

Arron became a mentor to young boys through coaching, and Chalese started volunteering at their church. They believed that by modeling generosity with their time, treasure, and talent, their children would have the greatest chance of living purpose-driven lives. The poisonous multigenerational malaise of entitlement that Arron saw in his extended family would not take root in the Lawrence household, and his children are already the better for it.

Journey into Conservatism

Arron's family grew, further changing his political perspective. As he considered matters like health care, taxes, education, and the family budget, Churchill's maxim came to fruition in his life.[1] The overwhelming sense that the destructive tentacles of government were too far-reaching became all the more evident.

As the 2016 election neared, a few things stood out to Arron regarding Donald Trump's candidacy. His positions on life, Israel, marriage, and family appealed to him. Trump's history of infidelity and vanity was irksome. At the same time, Hillary Clinton was as contrary to Arron's principles as she could possibly be. She was not somebody to trust; her record teemed with corruption and conflict.

Arron's vote became an issues-based vote. He believed that marriage was under attack. He believed that the most innocent were under attack. He believed that freedom of faith was under attack. He

---

1 "If you're not liberal at the age of 25, you have no heart, if you're not conservative at the age of 35, you have no brain."

believed that inner cities were worse after eight years of Obama policies.

Arron's dad still viewed the Republican Party as a detrimental force to the inner city. The belief that Republicans opposed minorities prevented him from voting for Trump. Yet, Arron found a sympathetic ear when speaking with his dad, who understood why Arron was prepared to swing his vote. They shared a conviction that the source of inner-city suffering is the welfare-dependent mindset of its people. Arron and his dad believed that the solution to this suffering is not the government. Instead, it is the transformation and revitalization of families' perspectives on welfare. Arron's experiences deeply changed his perspective and led him to vote exclusively on principle. In 2016 Arron cast his vote for Donald J. Trump.

Arron became a man of his own with a great foundation that allowed his faith to flourish. Despite their different voting records, Arron's father deeply instilled in Arron a conviction to act in accordance with principle. As a black man, Arron found it was Trump's stand on the *issues* that made him swing his vote. Arron believes that conservative philosophy will lead to inner-city flourishing. According to Arron, application of biblical values to one's life leads to prosperity, and the Republican platform best accommodates this perspective.

CHAPTER 4:

The Unspoken American Genocide

PREFACE

According to *Wall Street Journal* op-ed editor James Taranto, referencing historian Allen Guelzo, America was more divided in 2017 than it had been since the Civil War.[97] Taranto stopped short of suggesting a civil war was imminent, but he cited one issue that possessed the most potential to cause civil war: *abortion*. This word carries in its eight letters the stories of millions whose lives have become entangled in its treacherous web. Since *Roe v. Wade* (1973), 61 million babies have been aborted in America—and counting.[98]

Abortion recently grew more polarizing as Planned Parenthood (PP), the nation's largest abortion provider, was caught selling body parts of aborted babies. With millions of taxpayer dollars funding this enterprise, #defundplannedparenthood went viral. The pro-life movement seemingly gained momentum as candidates for office declared their commitment to act on that hashtag. Yet, at the time of this writing, Planned Parenthood continues to receive public funding from federal and state budgets.[99]

Why? How is it possible that such a vile enterprise could withstand such widespread attacks and reprisals? Into the ring stepped the Left. Modern-feminist organizations, Democratic politicians, public sector unions, human rights coalitions, and mainstream media came running to the defense of PP. Armed with MSNBC talking points, this movement continues to propagandize the idea that women's rights necessarily involve the right to abortion. Every woman stands to benefit, they argue, because their reproductive rights are on the line. Or are they?

With the advancement of modern science, more people are coming to recognize the inherent human nature of the baby in the womb.[100] As noted by pro-life Ashley McGuire, "When you're seeing a baby sucking its thumb at 18 weeks, smiling, clapping," it becomes "harder to square the idea that that 20-week-old, that unborn baby or fetus, is discardable."[101] People who convert from pro-choice to pro-life cross a major threshold toward conservative thought. To unlock the unalienable promises of liberty and the pursuit of happiness, *life* must first be considered unalienable.

My passion for early American history and its Founders led my wife and me to celebrate part of our ninth anniversary in Philadelphia. Among the many monuments we visited, one stood out: that of Harriet Tubman. Her story of bravery and sacrifice as a "conductor" on the Underground Railroad led to the salvation of hundreds of former slaves from bondage.[102] As I reviewed her brave story, I had an epiphany. The transition from pro-choice to pro-life is the underground railway for the millennial mind moving from left to right.

I had the privilege of meeting one such millennial who traveled this route, and who is now a conductor on the underground railroad to conservatism.

THE STORY OF **TIFFANY CRAIN**

Tiffany is a 37-year-old single mother of two from Perrysburg, Ohio. That Tiffany comes from a home where her mother and father's marriage remains intact makes her story even more surprising. Although Tiffany's parents attended church, they were not devout, nor did they require Tiffany to be. Politics was not to be discussed; this was a private matter in Tiffany's home. No party affiliation was mentioned. Often, her mother would reaffirm to Tiffany that she did not affiliate with any party but voted for candidates who fit her preferences. Consequently, Tiffany did not have a predisposition to either party.

Blank Slate

Life was normal for Tiffany: school, part-time jobs, boyfriends, and friends. Although she continued attending church, she rejected faith due to her uncertainty of its truth claims. Tiffany's mom was okay with this because of her own uncertainties. Yet this led Tiffany down a rebellious path and caused her to focus her teenage years on the distractions that so often plague teen lives.

Although she did not spend time thinking on most political issues, the life debate was inescapable. One distinct moment Tiffany recalls is choosing to debate on the pro-choice side during a sociology class. Beyond this issue, Tiffany's high school years were a pursuit of fleeting vanity, with grades as an afterthought. Graduation from high school seemed to awaken her to the recognition that she lacked direction and purpose. Thus, upon entry to Bowling Green State University, Tiffany decided that what she was missing was academic success.

Tiffany's renewed commitment to dive into academics caused her grades to soar. She met her academic goals. With a linear focus on academics, Tiffany did not have time to make many friends. That seemed okay at first; she was driven to succeed.

But then Tiffany came across people who caused a shift in her perspective. Tiffany met some girls in class who were different from any other young people she had met. These new friends lived with a vibrant faith, a faith that was central to their existence and determined the direction of their lives. Skipping class for events like Lent services made a deep and lasting impression on Tiffany.

Serendipitously, shortly after meeting these new friends, Tiffany was placed as a student-teacher at a religious school, St. Patrick of Heatherdowns. Her responsibilities included teaching the Gospels, which forced her to consider the truth of the existence of Jesus. By way of research, Tiffany became convinced the Bible was indeed true. Yet this recognition did not transfer from her mind to her heart. She continued living life as she always had. However impressed she was by her new friends, her old habits held sway over her.

In the meantime, in order to pay the bills, Tiffany worked a couple of jobs, including one as a nanny. She loved it. She loved it so much she decided to leave college and begin working as a full-time nanny. Her decision shocked those who knew her and knew of her drive for academic success. Yet her overwhelming love for children outdrove her old ambitions. Tiffany dreamed that someday she would become a mommy. Her willingness to sacrifice academic completion for something she loved foreshadowed the events to follow.

Politics and Compromise

While nannying, Tiffany eventually found herself in a relationship with a guy she thought she would marry. This relationship consumed her life. Suddenly, her boyfriend broke up with her, devastating her. Tiffany's sadness drove her to seek a community of loving people, which she found at church. Her non-work life filled up with mission trips to Haiti, leading Sunday school classes, and spending time with church friends. Nevertheless, Tiffany was uncertain as to how to apply faith to every aspect of her life, including her voting decisions.

During the rise of the Obama candidacy for president, Tiffany became caught up in the excitement and joined the masses to vote for the man who would become America's first black president. Tiffany's singular focus meant that she did not consider any of his policy positions, nor their ramifications. Her decision for Obama was based on pure emotion.

Although life went on as usual following Obama's 2008 victory, little did Tiffany know that her next relationship would change everything, including her political persuasion. When Tiffany met her next boyfriend, she was careful to explain her desire for a pure relationship. Her desire was to save sex for marriage. On their second date, Tiffany laid the ground rules, and her suitor responded, "I respect that." Looking back, she regrets failing to recognize that without a joint commitment to purity, these rules would be broken. Respecting a commitment is different from sharing a commitment.

The next year was an emotional struggle. Her boyfriend, who was living in Ann Arbor, Michigan, and preparing to move to Seattle, Washington, was not interested in marriage. Regularly the relationship would cascade to the point of breakup. A conversation and physical intimacy would ensue, papering over the couple's problems. The cycle continued, and the inevitable resulted: Tiffany got pregnant.

The Breaking Point

Tiffany's boyfriend had hidden much of his past, including that his ex-wife had had a couple of abortions. Had Tiffany known this, she might have been able to predict his response when she told him he was the father of her unborn child.

When she arrived at Ann Arbor to break the news, Tiffany's small hope of receiving comfort was dashed to pieces. Her boyfriend met her with condemnation and condescension. He accused Tiffany of getting pregnant in order to force him to marry her. He questioned her integrity, berating her for allowing this to happen. The meeting ended with him asking Tiffany a piercing question: *"What are you going to do about this?"* Her hopes of support ruined, Tiffany turned back for home, realizing the road ahead was nothing less than the valley of the shadow of death.

During the days that followed, Tiffany received increasing pressure from her boyfriend. He demanded an answer, covertly hinting at the "only thing to do." Soon, he began to overtly demand abortion. He helped set up a consultation with Planned Parenthood. Although Tiffany obliged because of her desire for his partnership, the consultation with America's leading abortion provider proved unconvincing. So, her boyfriend resorted to intellectual appeals. He began to call the baby in her womb "a clump of cells," absent of any meaning or purpose. As Tiffany struggled with morning sickness and the natural pains of pregnancy, she asked herself how it was possible for this to only be a clump of cells.

Meanwhile, Tiffany took the embarrassing and shameful steps of sharing her story with her church friends and pastor. Feeling like she was wearing a scarlet letter, Tiffany expected rejection and expulsion. However, in stark contrast to her boyfriend's response, she received overwhelming love and grace from her church. This group of people would become the anchor Tiffany needed to survive the intensifying storm.

As Tiffany pondered her options, life in the womb became a self-evident truth. The harder her boyfriend pushed, the greater her conviction became of her need to reject the destruction of her baby girl. Convinced that giving life was the right choice, Tiffany began to prepare for post-partum motherhood. Her first conversation in this direction was her most difficult. Returning to Ann Arbor, she had a glimmer of hope that she might change her boyfriend's mind, now that she had fully decided to give life.

For months he had expressed his desire for this child "to not be another statistic," referring to the fatherless rate of black youth in America. Tiffany decided he would have the opportunity to be a part of the change he yearned for. As she courageously began the conversation, she skipped the niceties. Tiffany explained her resolve to give their baby the life she already inherently possessed and explained that abortion was not an option. She then asked her boyfriend whether he would "man up" to ensure his baby would rise above the statistics that supposedly concerned him.

In this moment, Tiffany knew the response would determine the nature of her relationship with the father. Either he would step in and take responsibility, or he would selfishly abandon both mother and child. Without hesitation, his response was unequivocal: "It's me or the baby." She expected this answer, but it grieved her nonetheless. Yet she would not allow grief to alter her premeditated response. Tiffany turned away from her now *ex*-boyfriend, newly resolved to raise this baby in her womb without one iota of support from the father. As soon as she left, she called her church friends and asked them to pray. She was going to need it.

At Tiffany's next appointment, the ultrasound technician saw something that would shock her patient. Tiffany had been so sure she was growing a baby girl. In fact, she was growing twin boys.

This revelation bewildered Tiffany. Already feeling overwhelmed and isolated, Tiffany felt her responsibility was now doubly impossible. But she would not budge. Tiffany was resolved to be an incredible mom for two children—even boys.

At the next meeting with her Bible study group, Tiffany explained how her ex-boyfriend had given her the ultimatum, and then that she was going to have twins. Every single member of the group stated that even though the father did not want the babies, *they* did. A list was made, offering everything from childcare to baby cribs to car seats. Reminiscent of her college friends, these Christians lived their faith.

Throughout her pregnancy, Tiffany encountered unexpected support from these friends and others. Their support, counsel, and kindness were precisely what Tiffany needed to endure this difficult season. Their example would leave a lasting impression on Tiffany's life and approach to the issue of life. Eventually, the day came when Tiffany gave birth to two beautiful sons. The moment she saw their tiny feet, hands, and faces, she knew they were everything she had imagined. As she held her two baby boys, she was thankful she had not taken their little lives. Their fatherless future was no less bright than any other baby's in the ward. Indeed, Tiffany took to motherhood like a champion.

From Mommy to Mommy Counselor

Tiffany's transition back to work and childcare went as advertised. Yet, as difficult as it was being a single mom of two, nothing was more fulfilling than sacrificing to bring about her boys' success and purpose. She knew in her heart that her sons' trajectory was pointed toward greatness. Now with a full-time job, Tiffany experienced their first couple of years as a blur. But miraculously, every step of the way, Tiffany would find just enough provision, love, and care. Her boys were growing in a community of people who loved them and loved their mother.

The new mother's pace of life gave Tiffany little time to think about anything other than her job and her babies. The 2012 election season came and went without Tiffany giving it a second thought. The ramifications of her own story—of choosing life over abortion—had yet to sink in.

Things would not slow down for Tiffany until closer to 2015, when her boys were old enough to begin helping with some of the menial tasks that consume parental time and attention. About that time, a series of videos would rock her world. Two individuals had gone undercover among various Planned Parenthood employees, from senior executives to doctors to procurement technicians.[103] These videos revealed the graphic corruption and the inhumane perspective of these individuals.

According to Tiffany, one video showed an executive speaking recklessly about the baby's heart, ribs, and brain and how they were surgically amputated to be sold. It struck Tiffany as ironic that an organization that stands for women's rights would disregard a human's most essential right—the right to life. Tiffany spent hours going over these videos. The more she understood about the development of the baby—a heartbeat at 18 days, organ function at 8 weeks, fingerprints at 9 weeks, pain at 10 weeks, and a smile at 12 weeks—the more Tiffany became decidedly pro-life.[104]

Not long after, she began volunteering at a local pregnancy center. She refused to let her busyness, even as a single mom, prevent her from helping women and babies. Soon Tiffany was elbow-deep into something she adored. Much like her mentors from her church group, she invested her spare time counseling young women and giving them hope through her own story. For the first time in years, Tiffany saw her story as full of promise and hope for others. It was not long before the pregnancy center offered her a job.

Working full-time at the center, she met many young mothers and understood the crushing pressure many of them faced. Sometimes the pressure would come from their boyfriends and sometimes from their families. Many of the young ladies were college students who were told there was no way they could raise a child *and* succeed in life. Tiffany found great fulfillment as she helped each soon-to-be mom see the beauty of her baby. And many, like Tiffany, said yes to life.

The young mothers who refused her counsel occupied Tiffany's thoughts the most. She would often ponder whether there was something she could do to change the narrative of their communities for the sake of their babies. Many young ladies believed they would have little to no support from their families or boyfriends. The future of these babies lay in dire straits. Tiffany hoped to change that.

The Swing Vote

Meanwhile, the country was in full debate over who would become the next president. Hillary Clinton and Donald Trump were in the spotlight as the months led to November 2016. The previous eight years had changed Tiffany's perspective. The whirlwind of life-changing events made her a new person. Equipped with a new perspective, Tiffany approached the election of 2016 differently than in 2008.

No matter how much she liked or disliked a candidate or their party affiliation, one issue was paramount: *life*. In this election, it was easy for Americans to know who was pro-abortion and who was pro-life. Still, from each campaign emerged two perspectives that cemented Tiffany's swing from blue in '08 to red in '16. From the Clinton campaign, it was an unwavering commitment to both partial-birth abortion and America's number-one abortion provider: Planned Parenthood. From the Trump campaign, it was the creation of a list of potential Supreme Court justices from whom he would select a nominee. This list was praised by many as being full of justices who would defend the unalienable right to life.[105]

More than anything else, these two perspectives moved Tiffany to vote for Donald Trump. For the first time, Tiffany began to apply the full weight of her logic, experiences, and mentorship guidance in an election. In the past, Tiffany's opinion of a presidential candidate's qualifications had little to do with policy positions and much more to do with popular culture. Now, she looked past the image of the person and toward his or her principles.

Previously Tiffany followed the common leftist logic that Republicans are racist, but the further she looked into the issue of abortion, the more racism she saw on the other side. As a mother of mixed children, Tiffany was appalled by the number of black babies being aborted in America. As she studied history and investigated Margaret Sanger, the famed eugenicist and founder of Planned Parenthood, Tiffany recognized that Sanger targeted black babies in predominantly black communities.[106] Reflecting upon the possible fate of her sons, Tiffany learned that in New York City alone, there are thousands more black babies aborted than born.[107]

Many in Tiffany's circles were surprised and some were even appalled at Tiffany's position. In vain, she would try to logically convince her younger friends. Her most powerful tool, however, was more powerful than logic.

It was her story.

Many would try to debate fiercely with Tiffany about candidates and even the principle of life, until they heard her story. Instantly the combatant would turn into a gentle listener as this courageous young mother described why the principle of life is the first and most essential human right. In eight years, Tiffany had moved from an acquiescent liberal voter to a non-voter, and finally to a voter with conservative convictions. It was her own story of her twin boys that moved her.

The Rest of the Story

The passionate debate of a presidential election cycle is often eclipsed by the everyday challenges of everyday Americans. Tiffany is no different. Her dream to help young mothers was turning into a burning passion. With no experience leading a nonprofit, Tiffany launched "The Nest" in the spring of 2017. The Nest committed to providing early childhood education and daycare services to young families pursuing continued education, at no cost to the families.

Tiffany's vision was to change the false narrative of "abort your baby or abort your dream" into a new narrative of "give life to a baby and give life to a dream." She believed that if she could give birth to a new narrative, these young ladies, like her, would allow their babies not only to be born but also to fulfill their God-given potential.

It is one thing to dream a vision, however, and another thing to execute a vision. The work has been hard. Clearly, the word *quit* is not in Tiffany Crain's vocabulary.

With grit and hustle, Tiffany organized a board of directors, achieved tax-exempt 501(c)(3) status, acquired a building, and began offering services to mothers in the fall of 2018. At the time of this writing, The Nest is thriving. It is growing at an incredible rate and is serving a dozen families. Mirroring the generosity Tiffany received during her pregnancy, many individuals and churches in the Bowling Green area have given generously to The Nest. Due to the support from the community, the Nest will more than double in 2020, serving 28 families. Tiffany is a woman of action. Her story will impact many others because actions speak louder than words, and because story trumps debate. Tiffany's life-giving choice will give life to the dreams of children whose days are yet to be counted and to young mothers whose lives will bring about a dream they did not know was possible. Having successfully navigated the underground railroad of life, Tiffany is now a full-time conductor.

CHAPTER 5:
A Woman's Right to Defense

PREFACE

Type "gun violence" into Google, and you will find no end of tragic stories—and opinions on how to mitigate the collateral damage. The gun control debate rages in America. An outbreak of school shootings in early 2018 led to increasingly heated debate countrywide. Despite louder calls for gun control, it appears Americans increasingly favor firearms freedoms. According to a Pew Research report in June 2017, while only 30% of the population owned a gun, another 36% of adults who don't currently own one could see themselves owning one in the future.[108]

This trend is particularly notable among women, of whom many are victims of sexual violence in the United States, in which

1 in 4 women have been victims of severe physical violence by an intimate partner

1 in 5 women have been raped

1 in 7 women have been stalked by an intimate partner[109]

Citing gun control and domestic violence, the modern-day feminist movement is a champion for stricter gun laws. In their minds, fewer guns means less crime, including less gender-based violence. However, an increasing number of women reject this expression of feminism. A 2018 *Guardian* article investigated the new feminist movement supporting the right to bear arms for increased protection.[110] Former NRA spokeswoman Dana Loesch has argued specifically that arming women would help them defend themselves against sexual violence.[111]

Comparative analysis in places where access to guns is significantly diminished gives weight to this argument. Katie Pavlich notes,

"In Great Britain, where it's almost impossible to get a gun, a woman is three times more likely to be raped than in America, according to a study by David Kopel, a professor of constitutional law at Denver University."[112] Thanks to recent movements like #MeToo, the treacherous stories of sexual assault and victimization seem to parallel the sudden embrace of Second Amendment protections by women. According to the Crime Research Prevention Center, "between 2012 and 2018, the percentage of women with concealed gun permits grew 111% faster for women."[113]

As the debate continues to heighten, people of goodwill on both sides of the aisle pursue solutions to these heinous crimes. The polarity of these debates has led to far-reaching policy proposals to confiscate the guns of law-abiding citizens.[114] This total disregard for the Constitution has awakened many from the millennial generation to the extreme position of the Left. In 2016, one such millennial was awakened through the teachings of her father.

THE STORY OF **JENNA CLINE**

The moment Jenna walks into a room, the energy level rises. Her contagious personality is disarming, and her compassion quickly dissipates uneasiness. She is a people person. Emotionally intelligent, Jenna knows how to meet people where they are. A young millennial, she is a digital native, fluent in technology, and well connected. The combination of these  unique traits has led her to pursue a career in marketing.

Known as the "Coke Girl" while on campus, Jenna was the Ambassador for Coca-Cola at BGSU. Coca-Cola could not have selected a better person. Reaching out to thousands of students, Jenna was highly effective at building brand equity for Coca-Cola. Her flare, connectivity, and youthful vigor might lead one to predict she'd lean left politically, like many millennials on US campuses. But hidden under Jenna's contagious personality resides a considerable amount of wisdom derived from her family and her roots.

I met Jenna through an internship program. My company works with the state of Ohio to bring in some of Ohio's best and brightest through a program called the Ohio Export Internship Program (OEIP).[115] The OEIP selects and places a limited number of students at companies throughout Ohio. From day one, Jenna's contagious personality stuck out.

As the summer moved along, I had the chance to learn a little bit about Jenna and her story. Knowing how well connected she was on campus, I asked her if she knew of any students who had flipped their vote from Democrat to Republican in '16. She immediately volunteered herself as one such student. The more I learned of her story, the more convinced I became Jenna was emblematic of the rising demographic of young women who vote with gun rights as being central to women's rights.

Hearth and Home

Jenna is from small-town America. She points out that her rural Ohio hometown, New Madison, could easily have fit the idyllic small town from a romance movie. Even though she has experience living in large cities such as Charlotte, North Carolina, and even in Paris, France, Jenna's explanation of her hometown was filled with nostalgia. As the youngest of three girls, Jenna remembers a household always teeming with people and energy.

Jenna's dad, being from the Dayton area (near Wright-Patterson Air Force Base) had met her mom in New Madison while serving in the military. They quickly got married and, only three and a half years into his service, had their first daughter. The Clines would have two more girls over the next 10 years. Mr. Cline's military training was no match for the four ladies in his life. His instincts softened; he became the quintessential yes man to his girls. But if anything threatened his girls, his military instincts would come alive in no time.

Consequently, a major event occurred when Jenna was nine that would reactivate these instincts. One day, when the entire family was at school or at work, their house was robbed. The scare of robbery and the potential of his family's vulnerability changed Mr. Cline's perspective on home safety. The Clines sprang into action. They bought a dog and other security systems. Mr. Cline didn't stop there. He began to train his daughters in the use of firearms. From hunting to safety to shooting at the range, Jenna learned it all.

Jenna followed her dad in lockstep, but the gun safety intensity was not as popular with Jenna's older siblings. This disparity would create political differences in Jenna's family, although the Clines would remain closely knit together throughout the upcoming election season. Such differences might easily have driven the Clines apart.

2008 and 2012 Elections

Jenna was attentive to the 2008 elections during her middle school years. Her school worked exceptionally hard to make students aware of the United States' civic process. Through mock elections and in-class conversations, the teachers made the election a tangible part of education. In spite of its rural location, a large majority of Jenna's schoolmates were excited about Barack Obama. Obama would consistently win mock trials. New Madison's lack of racial diversity did not diminish their enthusiasm for the man who would become America's first black President. If New Madison's school systems would have determined the 2008 election, Barack Obama would have defeated John McCain with a larger margin than he actually attained in the general election.

In the Cline household, Jenna's sister was very pro-Obama. The most intellectually engaged member of the family, she proved instrumental in educating Jenna and Jenna's mom for this race. By contrast, Jenna's dad maintained conservative convictions and would not be swayed. Jenna's sister was confident and, thus, effective in her arguments of diversity and empathy for others. For the Cline household, this election would create more conversation than ever before about the need to expand their perspectives and look beyond New Madison to the impact that this election would have on other cities, states, and countries. Jenna was too young to vote, but in the unofficial ballot at school, she would vote in favor of Barack Obama.

Four years later, in 2012, the frequency of conversation surrounding the '12 election was significantly less than in '08. With Jenna's sisters now older and out of the house, Jenna and her parents did not carry forward the same vigor and passion from the '08 election. However, what was missing at home was thriving at school.

Jenna still supported President Obama, but her clarity of the *why* to vote for Obama had grown murky. Without her older sister to answer her questions, Jenna sought to educate herself. Unfortunately, most of the debate, especially around health care, confused Jenna. In contrast to the invincibility of the Obama campaign in '08, there were more students in '12 who voiced dissent. In the end, after much debate at school, Jenna decided to cast her vote in favor of President Obama. Now as she prepared to transition to a place with many more students on a larger campus with more diversity, her vote would be impacted but in the reverse direction.

The Move to Wood County

As Jenna began working toward high school graduation in a class of 59 students, she desired a place with more people, but also somewhere she could feel at home. An outstanding student, Jenna had many options, ultimately choosing BGSU as her destination. The campus in the heart of Wood County made her feel at home with cornfields surrounding the city.

Diversity, in demographic and in thought, was immediately evident. Her first roommate was from Cleveland, and their differences in living and in perspective were evident. To Jenna, this was rewarding, as diversity was one of the things she most desired from her college experience.

Among her many new friends, she gained one from California who was black and opinionated. The depth of their conversations gave Jenna newfound comprehension on a variety of topics, from drugs to incarceration to welfare. Jenna's friendship empowered her to compare her convictions with those of different people from different places. The friendly debate helped change some of her convictions while strengthening others. She would always seek to listen first to value the opinions of her friends, but listening did not always mean agreeing.

One issue on which Jenna strengthened her convictions was gun control. Deep conversations around the hurt and pain caused by guns seemed to shift blame from human beings who used inanimate objects to the inanimate objects themselves. From her vantage, gun control activists failed to understand that even if there are laws in place, people will still break the law. The idea that stricter laws will keep guns out of the hands of criminals was laughable. Gun laws most hurt the people who use guns responsibly. Jenna wanted people like her dad to have guns, because such people would never use guns maliciously. By contrast, somebody who has already broken the law will continue to break the law. Anti-gun laws thus give lawbreakers an advantage over innocent citizens.

Least convincing to Jenna was the argument that a woman would be safest in an environment of strict gun control. Her motivation to possess a license for carrying a concealed weapon (CCW) was the concern that dangerous people could harm her. For Jenna, if you take guns away, the criminals remain unchanged, and the most vulnerable have no defense. This logic strengthened her conviction that a woman's defense should not be compromised and that the Second Amendment was the safeguard for this defense. In a world where feminism is actively being debated, in Jenna's mind, women's safety must be central to that conversation.

Some of Jenna's friends argued that her personal safety motive was selfish. All around the country, innocent victims were losing their lives from gun violence. Jenna, being a compassionate person, considered this argument but found it lacking. Regardless of their weapons, criminals will always find victims. To truly protect victims, criminals themselves must be transformed. Rather than looking to gun control as a solution, Jenna looked further upstream in culture. She believed that stable families, communities, and the message of love would have the greatest impact. Breaking down barriers through conversation was essential. Government is not the answer to the school shootings and gun control laws; government is not going to change these shooters' minds. It takes faith, humanity, and love to change a life.

While having these conversations, Jenna developed a new community of friends at church. The transformational life-changing ingredients were found in the campus church she attended. It was at church where Jenna met people whose love was infectious. These people gave skin to the ideas that Jenna shared with her pro-gun-control friends. Their message of sacrifice and love led to the transformation of many lives. While laws protect, people transform. The people at her church helped to change Jenna's life through their faith. She believed this to be the ultimate answer to gun crimes raging throughout the country.

2016 Election

This season of conversation prepared Jenna for the 2016 presidential election and for her first official vote. While on BGSU's campus, Jenna was exposed to a Democrat political machine—In her classes, in the student union, in her clubs, and her dormitories. She couldn't escape the suffocating, canvassing campaign of the Hillary machine. Meanwhile, the Trump campaign and Trump fans were hardly visible on her campus, other than a few brave souls who were willing to be called bigots and racists.

Quietly, Jenna analyzed the candidates with precision and with concern. Trump's personality and his reckless messaging on social media concerned her. But for every concern about Trump's personality, she was equally concerned about Hillary's corruption, scandals, and seemingly sinister motives. Where Obama had stoked hope, Clinton stoked revenge and hate. In her mind, this election was going to be a choice between the lesser of two evils.

Regardless of her feelings on the "likeability" of the candidates, Jenna knew she needed to perform due diligence. She decided to give the race a fair and independent assessment. Her resolve to vote based on principle instead of personality was a shift from her approach during the '12 election, particularly when she got lost in the debate and simply supported Obama due to his personality. An independent assessment was not going to be easy. Many forces on campus sought to persuade, influence, and even intimidate her toward Hillary Clinton. Left-leaning professors, sororities, and other prominent feminist voices would lead a full-bore assault on masculinity. They would browbeat into submission any dissenting voice, championing women's rights through a simple comparison of the personalities of Donald Trump and Hillary Clinton.

Nevertheless, Jenna was resolved to ignore identity politics and to follow the logic of the arguments made by the campaigns. The presidential debates did not help Jenna make her decision. She felt like the debates were more about personality disputes than substantive policy debate. Campus voices sought to focus the blame on Trump for the debate fireworks, but Jenna looked with objective lenses and saw confrontation coming from both sides.

On campus, Jenna felt like spin and exaggeration were common communication strategies toward students. She noticed a level of blind hatred exacted toward Trump that was based on his personality. This hatred justified a blind usage of deceitful opinions and outright lies to delegitimize the Trump campaign. Cutting through the noise would prove a greater challenge than Jenna originally predicted. But she was up to it.

As is the case with most voters, the prism through which Jenna would determine her vote was complex and multifaceted. As a business major, Jenna was concerned about the state of the economy. As a millennial, Jenna was concerned about the growing intolerance shown toward conservative thinkers. As a person of faith, Jenna was concerned about racism and abortion. Finally, as a self-described feminist and the daughter of Mr. Cline, Jenna was concerned about women's safety—and, in her estimation, the right to bear arms appeared to be in danger.

Objective research led to a major surprise. Several times throughout the course of the debates and the campaigns, Clinton tipped her hand on the topic of gun control. There was no question that Clinton would leverage the immense power of the presidency to enact stricter gun laws. Not once did Jenna hear an argument from the Clinton camp assuaging her concerns of losing her options for self-defense. Hillary's narrative was exclusively focused on the danger of the guns, never on the danger of the criminals. By contrast, Trump was adamant in his defense of the Second Amendment and tough in his rhetoric toward criminals.

The contrast between the candidates' positions finally delivered the clarity Jenna needed to make her vote. Along with a small minority of students on BGSU's campus, Jenna decided to pull the lever in favor of Donald J. Trump. Leaving the ballot box, she did not regret this decision, but neither was it thinkable that Trump would win. To her surprise and to the dismay of many of her friends, her candidate pulled off the unthinkable upset.

Similar to the environment that one would experience at a funeral home, the day after the election, depression hung in the air on BGSU's campus. Many students quietly went about their business, but the dejection on their faces told all. Many of the students seemed to feel as if the end of our nation was imminent. For someone as upbeat and positive as Jenna, she could not help but try to encourage others. Her EQ prevented her from gloating and even from saying whom she voted for, but she did listen. Throughout the listening, she did not change her convictions. Jenna knew that policy trumps personality. Regardless of the media circus that would ensue, Jenna believed America was more secure and that even these depressed and dejected students would be better off.

The Future

Jenna Cline smiles at the future. With her newfound convictions intact, her barometer for choosing whom to support in an election gives her clarity. Like most other BGSU graduates, Jenna moved to another location to take a new job. Nevertheless, her experiences, her family, her friendships, and her newfound convictions will not be left behind. Similar to most millennials, she is not prepared to declare allegiance to any political party, but her journey has given her principled convictions to help her determine how to vote. Although the battle rages over gun control, Jenna will continue to vote for people who protect the vulnerable.

CHAPTER 6:
Faith Is Like Oxygen to Freedom

PREFACE

America has many heroes. Among them are famous names like Washington, Jefferson, and Lincoln. Not usually counted among them is George Whitefield (1714–1770). But this stocky five-foot preacher did more in four decades to change the soul of America than anyone who would follow. Because he undertook seven missionary journeys to colonial America from his home in England, an estimated 80% of colonial Americans heard Whitefield preach live.[116] His words challenged the colonists to become unchained from their religious encumbrances in Europe and to embrace a personal relationship with their Creator. A Great Awakening followed; it would shape the fabric of American society for years to come. Importantly, it would birth independence in the soul of the colonists, ultimately leading to their independence of mind, as declared in the Declaration of Independence.

Simply put, absent Whitefield's impact on colonial Americans and the Church, America would not have declared independence in 1776.

America has become less religious since the days of Whitefield. Consider recent drops in church attendance. Gallup began to track church attendance in 2008 at 42%, with it dropping to 38% in 2017.[117] The trend is even more pronounced among millennials. An estimated 23% of Generation X Americans claim no religious affiliation, but this rises to 34% among millennials born between 1981 and 1989, and to 36% among millennials born between 1990 and 1996.[118] Such statistics have led to bold declarations among the Left, like the one made by Harvard Law Professor Mark Tushnet in 2016: "The culture wars are over; they lost, we won."[119]

As society and culture have shifted left, the frequency of name-calling, persecution, and outright attacks on people of Judeo-Christian faith seems to have increased in America.[120] The Left has doubled down on its efforts to isolate people of faith as lunatics, bigots, and racists. Simply Google the words "white Christian America," and you'll find a bunch of articles on leftist sites like *Vox*, *NPR*, and *The Atlantic*. Each supposes America to be Christian and supposes Christians to be white. Such statements made by mainstream media and leftist intellectuals from ivory towers are one thing—but what is the true state of the Christian faith in swing-country America? Does faith still make a difference, or is it no longer relevant in a post-truth culture?

THE STORY OF **ALFONSO MACK**

The first time I met Alfonso was on BG-SU's campus at an information meeting for students interested in going on a missions trip to volunteer with the nonprofit I founded, Champions in Action. My brother Joe, a former basketball player at BGSU, along with my own history as a former football player, enabled us to have a platform for athletes. Thus, the room was filled with student-athletes from multiple sports.

From the moment I met Alfonso, I knew he was special. Showing deference to those around him, his humility was evident. Alfonso became one of eight students who decided to raise support and make the trip to Guatemala to serve at-risk youth. Because Alfonso was a walk-on with bills to pay, his decision was not inconsequential. Yet Alfonso felt that God would provide for his step of faith. I am grateful he made that sacrifice, because it allowed me to build a relationship with an individual of incredible influence. His instant connection with the at-risk boys in Guatemala foreshadowed a future filled with the ministry of service to others.

Good Kid

Alfonso grew up in inner-city South Bend, Indiana. His family had ideas of faith, but they weren't true believers. They would pray at night, but this habit was purely cultural. The only times they would enter a church building were on Easter and Christmas. One year, however, a radical transformation occurred in Alfonso's mom's life. She became a Christian when Alfonso was 8 or 9. She stopped cursing and drinking, and she started regularly attending church.

It was at this point that Alfonso gained a moral thought process. He believed that as long as he did good, he would make it to heaven. He thought, "If I could avoid drinking, cursing, and sex, I could make it to the pearly gates." He heard the gospel preached but did not understand it. Even though he could see his mom living it out, it did not reach him. Nevertheless, he had some incredible experiences, such as being released from porn and masturbation at the age of 15. As his mom and uncle began to pray for him, he was delivered. His heart changed.

Alfonso has one full little sister and three half-siblings: one older brother, one older sister, and one younger brother. Alfonso and his younger sister lived at home. His parents separated around the time when his mom accepted Christ. Consequently, his dad was often not around. Mom ran a tight ship. She set tight curfews and tough boundaries. Alfonso and his siblings wouldn't dare cross her, for fear of discipline.

Alfonso's schooling experience was unique because he chose a high level of academic rigor. Therefore, his closest peers were generally positive and stable. But outside of this peer group, most of the students were vulnerable to negative influences. They were angry, self-absorbed, involved in gangs, and hostile. Although Alfonso never experienced personal violence, he did experience some crime when some of his neighbors—high-school peers—robbed his house. These neighbors were dangerous. A few days later, one of them killed another over a game of dice.

Alfonso was generally a good kid. When he did succumb to peer pressure, his conscience nagged him. Due to his good nature, avoidance of vice, and church attendance, he gained a reputation as the "church boy." People generally respected him because he was a constant in an unstable environment.

Football had already become a major influence in Alfonso's life by the time he reached high school, but not for the love of football. Undersized, Alfonso played not because he was good but because he loved being with his friends. Several of his friends were stars on the field and were popular at school. The outcomes of these childhood stars would vary greatly. One friend later lost his way, falling into gangs and drugs and violence in high school, although eventually, he would repent. Another friend went on to graduate and play in the NFL. This friendship would prove consequential for Alfonso's future.

Once Alfonso was promoted to starting cornerback during his sophomore year, the game itself hooked him. Alfonso became a full-time starter in his junior year and a two-way starter his senior year. His reputation grew in the city as his game improved. His stardom immediately expanded his peer base beyond his high school to other schools. Shockingly to Alfonso, many positive externalities resulted from this success.

Unexpectedly, his football success helped him cement a relationship with his dad. A restaurant owner, Alfonso's dad would hear the praises heaped upon his son while other kids were bemoaned for squandering their potential. Due to divorce and work, his dad was only semi-involved at home, but he loved his kids. Now, Alfonso's dad not only loved him—he also respected him. Their conversations matured, and their relationship deepened. Naturally, Alfonso's worldview and self-worth became shaped by his success on the field.

But collegiate offers to play football were few and far between. Only one Division II school pursued him heavily. At the last minute of the recruiting deadline, a Division I team finally expressed interest: BGSU. The reason for their interest was because of another one of Alfonso's long-time teammates. Through film review of this teammate, the coaches saw some potential in another player on the field who caught their attention.

Alfonso was offered the opportunity to be a preferred walk-on at BGSU, which meant he would have to work extra hard to be noticed. Naturally, he came with a chip on his shoulder. When he arrived at BGSU during the summer of 2012, he knew what to expect. His high school coaches in South Bend were former Division I and NFL football players who had made sure Alfonso was fully aware of the challenge of being a walk-on at a Division I football program. Football was about to become the master of his schedule, relationships, and even his identity.

Election Day 2012

As Alfonso transitioned from two-a-day workouts into a more sustainable regimen during the school year, the last thing on his mind was the upcoming presidential election. Yet, here he found himself, in 2012, as an 18-year-old at BGSU, and he met several people asking him to register as a voter. At that point in his life, his barometer for elections was nothing more than image, race, and personality. In his distant memory, Alfonso remembered watching a debate in middle school between McCain and Obama. Alfonso knew that minorities would largely vote Democratic, but he had no idea why. He had met only one politician in his life and had zero political awareness. The only thing that excited Alfonso, and an overwhelming majority of his peers, was the race of Obama. Although there were a few families of color who didn't like Obama, Alfonso did not know why. Most of Alfonso's classmates and teammates believed that having a black president was the only issue of importance.

There were people on campus who drove golf carts that would take people to register and vote. These individuals from the university were seemingly ever present during the month leading up to Election Day. Ohio, with some of the most lenient early-voting laws, made it incredibly easy for students like Alfonso to cast their vote. Finally, one afternoon, he decided to take advantage of the opportunity. Although Alfonso does not recall exactly how he voted down the ticket, he knows exactly how he voted at the top: for Barack Obama.

Freshmen had more time on their hands than their older teammates, especially when the team was traveling. Consequently, on November 6, 2012, Alfonso and his roommate were able to watch the election results in his dorm. Many people of diverse backgrounds on his floor were also present, and there was a buzz of excitement as the results poured in. Alfonso thought it amazing that President Obama was doing a good enough job to be re-elected into office. But as soon as the election was over, Alfonso would think very little about the election. His mind was on other things.

College Years

As noted, being a football player at the Division I level is all-consuming. Life revolves around football. Although Alfonso was not surprised by the amount of time and effort required, he did not deny its difficulty. He resolved to keep his grades up. Alfonso knew what it took to get good grades, but he needed to find a way to adjust his schedule to have more freedom to make decisions. Adjust he did, as he would eventually graduate with an astounding 3.96 GPA, magna cum laude.

Then, in the spring after the election, Alfonso pulled both hamstrings and could not compete. His coaches threatened to kick him off the team unless he dedicated himself to staying in Bowling Green over the summer to train with the team. His commitment to follow his coaches' advice paid off. As he entered his sophomore season, everything turned to Alfonso's favor, as many of the cornerbacks dropped out due to injury. He was finally able to join the 60-man travel squad, thereby solidifying his spot on the roster. Alfonso was overjoyed at finally being recognized for his talent. His life was driven by football, but for the first time, something bigger emerged.

One player named Ronnie talked to Alfonso about authentic faith. Ronnie lived the faith he proclaimed, and it was Ronnie's authenticity that most convicted Alfonso. Ronnie was all-in with his faith; Alfonso was not. The primary area of his life he refused to relinquish control of was relationships with women. One moment would change that. After winning the Mid-American Conference (MAC) Championship, Alfonso spent the night with a girl for the first time. However, God was working on him, and the entire night he had no desire to physically engage, due to guilt and shame. His conscience burned within him, even though nothing physical had happened. This was a sign. When he woke up the next morning, he resolved to go all-in, like Ronnie.

The next semester, Alfonso was a new man. Fully committed to the gospel, his perspective on life changed. His heart for the Lord was ablaze. He dove into the Scriptures and sought to serve with everything he had. Everything in his life was redeemed. Even the idol of football had to bow down to Alfonso's Savior. For the first time in his life, he felt free. Free from the world's expectation, from football's condemnation, free from the vices of sin, and free to live a life of purpose and intentionality. Faith brought freedom into Alfonso's life, and its ramifications were tremendous.

During spring ball, Alfonso fought with everything he had to try and get the starting spot, but with a new coaching staff, all the traction and credibility he had gained was lost. However, instead of letting this hurl him into depression, Alfonso decided to dig deeper into his faith. He traveled to Guatemala as a volunteer in the summer of 2014, which is where I (the author) met Alfonso. Traveling to Guatemala radically changed his perspective. When he saw children who lived with joy in the midst of significant poverty, it shook him. He realized he had much to be grateful for, and that sports gave him a platform to be used for God's greater glory.

When Alfonso returned to Bowling Green that summer, he was on fire. Alfonso did what he could to share the gospel with his teammates while trying to succeed on the field. He grew in strength and speed. He could squat over 540 pounds and could run a 4.4-second 40-yard dash. Everything was feeling good, and he believed he was headed right into a starting position.

But things rarely go the way that we expect. The new coaches, rather than promoting Alfonso, demoted him to the scout team. To make matters worse, Alfonso got injured. The depth of his faith was challenged, and he soon began to question God as to why he was struggling so much on the field. It was not long before Alfonso began to consider quitting the football team. One of his God-fearing teammates then challenged him on the centrality of his faith. Clearly, his instinctual response was governed by an identity rooted in football and not in Christ.

Someone challenged Alfonso to read Tim Keller's book *The Prodigal God*. This book shook him to his foundation, and he repented of his sin. Serendipitously, it was around this time that he met a speaker at a Fellowship of Christian Athletes (FCA) event. The speaker had experienced the same exact situation as Alfonso while playing at Youngstown State. He had quit during his third year because his coaches weren't playing him. This speaker said that he regretted quitting his team and told Alfonso that he believed the primary reason he was speaking at this event was to encourage Alfonso not to quit. He also challenged Alfonso to use football to share the gospel with his teammates, regardless of the outcome of the ballgame. This encouragement changed Alfonso's perspective as it related to football.

Alfonso decided to stay on the team and, miraculously, was promoted back to the travel squad the next week, and he finished the year contributing on special teams.

During his fourth year, his redshirt junior year, Alfonso burned for Christ. Teammates were reaching out to him to learn about his faith. Meanwhile, during a game against Maryland, Alfonso had a breakout game and would be promoted to starter. By the end of the season, he ranked seventh in the country in interceptions, he won a MAC Championship, and he was projected to be drafted in the third round of the NFL draft. But rather than going into the draft, the words of the FCA speaker remained in his spirit; he had more work to do with his teammates, so he decided to stay his senior year.

During that all-important senior year, Alfonso's influence was cemented. Not one individual among the 104 other players on the roster failed to recognize his leadership. Unexpectedly, however, he had to deal with another coaching change. His coaches had been so successful that they were recruited to Syracuse, leaving the program in the hands of new coaches. The transition in leadership at the top would turn the world of the players upside down. The success they had experienced the previous four years was to become a thing of the past, and Alfonso would have to learn to lead through a losing season.

Not only were the losses happening in the W/L column: Alfonso also lost his starting position to younger players. The coaches, after seeing no prospect for success that season, decided to invest in the future, leaving Alfonso on the bench. Although devastated by the loss of playing time, Alfonso responded true to his new form. He committed further to the advice of the FCA speaker, and he decided to invest in his teammates. No longer was Alfonso's identity bound to his football status. He shared hope freely. A legacy was therein built as his teammates would never forget his impact on their lives. At one FCA event that season, all five BGSU players speaking testified to it, specifically naming Alfonso as a mentor.

2016 Election Cycle

Compared to the relative freedom of 2012, Alfonso was so busy with football in 2016 that he did not have any time to vote. Now, four years older and having his perspective on life transformed by faith, he no longer looked at anything in life through the same lens. More important than any other identity—be it racial, athletic, political, or familial—Alfonso was a Christian first. Everything else was to be submitted to this framework, including which presidential candidate he would support in 2016.

Alfonso had decided he would base his vote on neither the race nor the personality of the candidate. He sought to center his voting decisions on *principle*, with the Bible as his standard. The timing of the newfound perspective came during a difficult election cycle. Neither candidate checked all of the boxes. He had concerns about the integrity of Donald Trump and questioned much of his past. At the same time, Hillary Clinton seemed to lack integrity by virtue of the many scandals that had plagued her throughout her political career. The difference-maker for Alfonso, true to his reframed perspective, was Hillary's platform. The nail in the coffin was the full embrace of abortion and her opposition to religious freedom in favor of the LGBT agenda. Although Alfonso was unable to cast a vote during the 2016 election cycle, in four years, faith had swung his voting preferences.

Election Day fell on a day the team was traveling to Northern Illinois to play a game. While traveling, Alfonso and his teammates were able to watch the results. Polling predictions had set expectations even among the least politically engaged—in this case, a football team. As the likelihood increased that Donald Trump could win the presidential election, the team was shocked. However, to Alfonso's surprise, his teammates weren't upset. For the most part, they accepted Trump as president, and a majority even preferred him over Hillary.

Post-Game Analysis

Now married and serving as a rising pastor at a campus church in Bowling Green, Alfonso has reordered his life, including his politics, entirely around his faith. In a culture where everything has been deemed Right or Left, Alfonso's frame of reference is Up and Down. He remains uncertain of the truth in matters like immigration, justice, and welfare—so, Alfonso uses Scripture to discern what and whom to support.

Although the Left has deemed this population as irrelevant, in swing-country America, Christian millennials are a force to be reckoned with. Millennials like Alfonso Mack vote with a new frame of reference because of their faith. But they also *love* with a new frame of reference because of their faith. It is this nonpolitical, selfless love—based in truth—that gives this demographic the greatest chance for growth and influence in the age to come.

CHAPTER 7:

Free Enterprise Is to Compassion as Socialism Is to Oppression

PREFACE

Recently, Ben Sasse, the junior US Senator from Nebraska, wrote a book entitled *The Vanishing American Adult: Our Coming-of-Age Crisis*. According to Sasse, the statistics are daunting: 30% of college students drop out after their first year, and only 4 in 10 graduate. One in three 18-to-34-year-olds lives with his or her parents.[121] Increasingly throughout the United States and in European countries, young people are working less and becoming more dependent and more entitled.

Entitlement has become the status quo and has poisoned the minds of younger generations. In the welfare state, taking care of yourself is no longer a virtue. The entitlement mentality eventually leads to the erosion of civil rights, as dependence always comes with greater government regulation. Government is no longer instituted to protect God-given unalienable rights. It is now an active agent that provides for our every need.

Which, of course, is a promise no government can keep.

Government, which is simply a proxy term for *power*, is a terrible agent for giving. The more a government increases in scope, the more the freedoms of the individual are reduced. Socialism's rising popularity among the millennial generation is a natural downstream consequence of the entitlement mentality.[122] This mentality is short-sighted and dangerous. Experience has shown that socialism is a destructive force leading to human suffering. The once-lauded leader of Venezuela, Hugo Chavez, led his nation down the path of socialism. As a result, Venezuela has become a cauldron of human suffering with government control of everything.

America would need to abandon its essence were it to embrace socialism. Socialism produces selfish people who complain instead of producing heroes who sacrifice. The more the millennial recognizes socialism for what it truly is—and the more that millennials meet people who have been poisoned by socialism—the more they will embrace free enterprise.

THE STORY OF **DOUGLAS SIMPSON**

Douglas Simpson is on the younger side of the millennial demographic. His youthful vitality is evident almost immediately upon meeting him. Doug's disarming conversational style and grasp of history would have made him a tremendous asset for the Left. Yet it was this very same understanding of history that would ultimately sway him to the Right. His former passionate embrace of socialism could be matched only by his swift and total rejection of it.

Growing up in the Akron, Ohio, area, Doug had a good childhood. Both of his parents were present and involved. Never forceful, his parents were always supportive. His family was considered to be middle or working class. His dad came from a poor family of eight who barely scraped by, and his mom was middle class and college educated. Once his dad and mom married, they were able to jointly ensure that their children would not suffer in poverty. Doug's parents spared nothing to secure a comfortable situation for their children. Doug cannot remember his parents withholding anything of necessity, and even more impressive was the savings they amassed for his college education.

Doug's dad used to work at a newspaper company as a mechanic to keep the machines running. He is scatterbrained, focused on the moment, and charismatic. True to the maxim "opposites attract," Doug's mom is soft-spoken, frugal, and reserved. Neither of Doug's parents was political, and they did not discuss politics as Doug was growing up.

Doug was a good student, but school bored him. The stuff he really enjoyed had to be read outside of school. Consequently, he read for leisure as often as he could. He and his dad shared a love for war movies and history, especially military history. Although Doug's parents did not talk politics, Doug did know that both his parents voted in '08 for Obama. His dad flipped his vote to Romney in '12, but his mom always voted Democratic. As for Doug, it wouldn't take long for his fledgling political persuasions to ignite.

Few kids Doug's age shared his love for history, and fewer still were interested in gleaning from Doug's ever-increasing knowledge. Despite his peers' widespread disinterest in politics, however, they recognized a level of brilliance in Douglas Simpson; many speculated public office would be in his future. In his sophomore year of high school, politics and government started to interest Doug.

Doug's foray into politics and government began with his reading of the *Communist Manifesto*. This book prompted him to consume additional socialist materials, including books like *Socialism Unbound*. Doug soon became an edgy teen, seeking to overthrow the rich class (bourgeoisie) and devouring leftist books, podcasts, and media. It wasn't long before knowledge turned into action. Doug became involved in bipartisan campaign finance reform at age 17. He started by calling people and talking to state representatives and state senators. After a few months, he was asked to become a leader, including making presentations for training activists. The group's primary cause was to get a constitutional amendment through an Article V Convention of the States in order to secure campaign finance reform.[123] Doug felt as if the movement was gaining momentum until he met with the state senator from his district, who, after 30 seconds, said no and gave an unrelated excuse. The inability to garner support from members of the Ohio House and Senate led to the downfall of the project and to Doug's departure from this group. But a fire had been lit.

As he consumed socialist content, Doug became more convinced that the working class was being exploited by rich capitalists. Doug's compassion attracted him to socialism because of its hypothetical ability to provide for everyone's basic needs. Yet, despite his socialist convictions in the realm of economics, Doug had convictions about the First and Second Amendments. He believed freedom of speech to be an essential right, and he believed people must have the right to defend it. Recognizing a contradiction between state-owned property (including weapons) and the Second Amendment right to bear arms, Doug reconciled that the state would just need to license guns to its people to protect the freedom of speech. Looking back, he would come to realize the absurdity of this idea. How could a government with absolute power arm a population whose possession of arms would threaten the government's absolutism? Doug later noted that in Venezuela, the government licenses weapons specifically to groups who support the government, with the sole intent of increasing abuse, threats, rape, and torture of opposition groups.[124] Doug would later lament that First Amendment rights cannot be protected when might makes right.

Journey to Awakening Begins

Fully engaged in his socialist-leaning political activities, Doug wasted no time preparing for Akron University. By the time Doug graduated from high school, he had already taken some college courses and had one year of credits. So, Doug plunged right into the core classes for his preferred major: political science. No one who knew him back home was surprised by his choice. But his choices that arose from this major would surprise everyone—Doug most of all. Doug was about to meet the people who would cause him to flip from blue to red, from socialist to capitalist, from big government to small government.

At Akron University, Doug knew he had found a home among his peers. He finally knew people his age who would tackle topics he was passionate about. A proponent of free speech, Doug gravitated toward people willing to debate him. He quickly developed a core group of friends who would last throughout his collegiate education. One of these friends was a veteran who had been deployed previously and was an avowed libertarian. Being naturally curious, the veteran visited college political groups of every stripe. This friend's exposure generated an unusual depth of conversation with Doug, expanding Doug's worldview. Another friend of Doug's was a radical socialist. The socialist was sharp and confident in his position. Initially, Doug was naturally attracted to this friend, given the similarities of their worldviews. Often, the libertarian would debate the socialist. Over time, the veteran's arguments became more persuasive to Doug.

Doug's veteran friend lived as he believed. He was very individualistic, yet extremely cognizant of others. He lived with fierce independence but was meek. He was a "live and let live" kind of guy. On the topic of free enterprise, he argued that if you hate poverty, you should love capitalism. Using data, the veteran showed that as countries move away from socialism, their people flourish. One memorable data point that influenced Doug was that worldwide wealth had increased significantly over the past 40 years because of free enterprise.[125] Through increased diversity of books, podcasts, and speakers with a libertarian perspective, Doug was exposed to powerful counterarguments to the socialist agenda.

A Deep Dive into Socialist Leadership

While building a relationship with the veteran, though, Doug spent an equal amount of time getting to know his socialist friend. And much of what the socialist offered in debate Doug understood already. Slowly, Doug began to see flaws both in the premises of socialism as well as in the lifestyle embodied by those who supported it, including his socialist friend. For example, coming from a working-class family, Doug expected socialism's intellectual champions to live like him. Much to his chagrin, his newfound socialist acquaintances were quite the opposite. Everything these friends did exhibited wealth, including regular $5 lattes, expensive clothes, and nice cars. Living off the bounty of their parents, these friends preached one message, but they lived another. His socialist friend came across as elitist, placing Doug among his proletariat pupils in need of his sage advice. The more he listened to his friend, the more Doug felt inferior to his socialist friend. In every conversation, there was an obvious implication: "I am better than you; therefore, you must submit to my ideas."

Finally, Doug became exhausted at the obvious contradiction and confronted his rich, socialist friend. Doug challenged him to disparage his wealth if he truly felt that capitalism was evil. In a statement as ridiculous as it was hypocritical, his friend's defense was that he was fighting capitalism with capitalism.

Initially, challenges like these were fair game with his socialist friend, so the relationship continued. However, his friend grew more radicalized once he began dating a revolutionary girlfriend. Conversations turned toxic; the friendship frayed. At one point, his socialist friend began to post radical statements online. He once posted, for example, that people would need to die in order to bring about the revolution. Doug and his group of friends confronted the socialist and stated that his thought processes were both radical and dangerous, but to no effect. Doug had to leave him behind, even though he had not yet quite gotten rid of his own socialist persuasions.

One person who helped to influence Doug's departure from socialism was a narcissistic socialist girl. According to Doug, she was a stereotypical Bernie Sanders supporter, drinking $5 lattes every morning on daddy's credit card while ignoring the homeless person right next to her. She was a leader for a leftist political group in the area, which is how Doug met her. She had a massive ego and would exercise it toward others, including Doug. Once again, Doug was somehow deemed inferior by ardent socialists in his circle. Although strong in opinion and fierce in debate, this socialist leader lacked the fortitude to practice what she preached. Even the smallest of tasks that required some level of effort and responsibility were considered by her to be "adulting." Her lifestyle was not compatible with the beliefs she espoused.

The more Doug studied history, and the more socialists he met, the more concerned he became. He began to recognize a pattern he calls "the fall of leadership": the closer a person is to being a centralized leader, the more narcissistic he or she becomes. Doug began to investigate the personal lives of those leaders with absolute power, including the likes of Mao, Hitler, and Saddam Hussein. For example, leaders in socialist countries would force agricultural mechanization on their citizens. They would kill horses and replace them with machinery, but once the horses were killed, government incompetence led to a limited supply of tractors. Farmers, desperate for the ability to produce and survive, needed to create a black market for horses. Yet as the people's suffering increased, these socialist officials would never admit their fault, choosing to punish the very farmers they were "saving." Doug saw this flaw in history's leaders, and now he saw it in his contemporary socialistic friends. The key issue for Doug came down to ego. The more consolidated the power without checks and balances, the more ego would thrive, and the more corruption would increase.

The 2016 Primary and Doug's Transition

The flurry of these relational storms occurred during the spring of 2016, the heart of primary season. Doug, having always been a staunch

Democrat, voted for Bernie Sanders in the primary. But the more he studied socialist leaders of the past in comparison with socialist leaders of the present, the more this historical comparison would serve as the nail in Doug's socialist coffin. Convinced individuals can and should make the decisions that best suit them, Doug sought leaders and leadership models that dissipated authority instead of concentrating it. The power of self-determination being what Doug most desired, he began to reconsider his political convictions. Then, having rejected socialism, Doug did not know where to turn. Voting for a Republican was against his nature, or so he thought.

In July 2016, Doug's faithful veteran friend invited him to a speech at the RNC in Cleveland. The speech and intellectual brilliance of many Doug met at the convention impacted his psyche.

In stark contrast to Doug's socialist friends, the veteran practiced what he preached. He became the primary influencer of Doug's beliefs. Being around those at the convention reversed many of Doug's preconceived notions about Republicans. He met people from many walks of life, rich and poor, young and old, black and white, but all passionate about the Republican Party. Coupled with powerful principles, these people reversed Doug's hesitation to join the Republican ranks. A month later, Doug dove in wholeheartedly. He became the College Republicans treasurer at Akron University and would end up volunteering with them from '16 to '18.

In spite of his newfound political philosophy, in '16, Doug was hesitant to jump on the Trump train, uncertain if he could vote for him. He had concerns with Trump's past and with how he communicated. On the other hand, he liked his vision for deregulation and preferred his experience as a businessman as opposed to that of a politician. And Trump's wealth and fame, prior to politics, meant that he likely wouldn't need the White House to accumulate more wealth and fame. Meanwhile, Doug doubted Hillary Clinton's authenticity. He felt she was 100% fake, from her image to her communication. No matter what, Doug could not vote for Clinton—but could he vote for Trump?

It took until three weeks before the election to make a decision. This was the first time Doug had ever voted in a presidential election, and he was convinced the only viable candidate was Donald Trump. Uncertain as to how he would feel flipping his vote from Sanders to Trump in only six months, Doug closely monitored his feelings *the day of*. To his surprise, he felt good leaving the voting booth, but he did not believe Trump was going to win. Throughout the day, the Democrats on campus were making fun of the Republicans. Initially dejected, Doug and his friends grew more and more elated throughout the course of the day. Soon, it was the Republicans celebrating the victory.

Throughout the election, Doug's dad became more convinced of Trump's platform. As was the norm in the Simpson household, there was little talk and even less persuasion one way or the other. Doug's mom supported Clinton, but only because she did not like Trump. After deciding to vote for Trump, Doug sought out his dad for deeper conversation; indeed, they began to cheer together for a miraculous Trump victory. Doug's mom, always the good sport, was happy for her son, but she was not going to let him gloat without at least playing a practical joke. Doug's parents' lawn, decorated with a Trump sign, had been vandalized with spray paint crossing out Trump's name and replacing it with Clinton. Leaving his home to return to campus the night of Trump's stunning victory, Doug noticed the vandalized sign. He ran in to tell his parents and found his mother laughing hysterically at the look on his face. She confessed to being the vandal. True to form, the Simpson family remained unified regardless of political outcomes, and election night 2016 was no different.

Life as a Conservative

In spite of Doug's newfound allegiance with the College Republicans, Doug's veteran friend still insisted they visit the other groups on campus. During conversations, they would engage with College Democrats, socialists, and other special interest groups to discuss the results of the 2016 election. Most of these conversations were civil and, in most cases, these groups wanted their guests to explain what they needed to do in order to win future elections.

Even though they had good conversations, many of the students could not begin to imagine how anybody could vote for Trump. According to Doug, it was like describing the color red to a color-blind alien. Akin to Doug during his years as a socialist, these students were captivated by their community and worldview. Change would take time, but Doug and his veteran friend were able to gain valuable insight into their mindset and meet people who would continue to shape Doug's journey into conservatism.

One of those individuals was a Venezuelan student Doug met in the spring of '17. Although Doug grappled with the rich and racist stigma associated with capitalists, he sought living examples to demonstrate what he believed to be true. His Venezuelan friend's life experience would bring life to the greatest fears associated with a system that squeezed the life out of society.

Before Venezuela nosedived into poverty and starvation, its government, under the leadership of Hugo Chavez, was elevated on a global platform as an outstanding model of socialism. Chavez was lauded as a courageous leader who would stand up to the big American bully. Many were the American detractors who praised Venezuela as a rising power while disparaging America as a "has been."[126] However, as is the case with totalitarian governments with closed economies and socialist policies, Venezuelans would soon begin to suffer severe poverty.

Doug's Venezuelan friend survived because his mom braved the system, finding ways to overcome great obstacles. The pressure of the iron-fisted government forced submission and support. She disagreed with Hugo Chavez's politics, but she knew she would need to fake support to ensure survival for her son. Thus, she would publicly express her support for Chavez, and she began to network with Chavez officials. It wasn't long before she was offered an opportunity in the government as an HR supervisor. As she rose in the ranks, she began making hundreds of thousands of dollars working for the government. Her job was 100% based upon her public support of the Hugo Chavez political platform. Performance on the job was irrelevant. Often, she would take her son to rallies and fake support of Chavez to retain her employment. However, as the Venezuelan economy imploded, inflation devastated her earnings and led her into poverty. She would lose more money working than spending her time bartering in the black market. Living in poverty and under the continual threat of death, she found a way to survive in the black market due to the many relationships she gained working for the government.

Despite overwhelming challenges, she would receive a glimmer of hope through her son, who became Doug's friend. In 2015, Doug's Venezuelan friend received a miraculous ticket of freedom to enter the US on a student visa before things went south. His life in the US would now be committed to studying, supporting his mom, and sharing about the evils of socialism. His experience has led him to extol America as a beacon of hope. Nobody believes in American exceptionalism more than Doug's Venezuelan friend. Whenever entitled elitist youth extol the virtues of socialism, his story shuts them down.

Once Doug could put skin to the greatest fears of socialism, his convictions for conservatism grew. As a champion for the working class, Doug knew there was no better model for their success than the free-enterprise system of America. His transition to conservatism was motivated by the conviction that this worldview was the best hope for all Americans in every class. The more Doug studied history and met friends like this Venezuelan, the more he saw a trend of toxic government intervention damaging to nearly everything in its path.

Now, when Doug debates friends, his first objective is to give people hope. He knows that hope cannot come from elitist, power-hungry leaders; it must come from transcendent truths and unalienable rights. To that end, as Doug transitioned out of college, he committed his life to sharing the gospel of free enterprise to groups throughout Wood County, Ohio.

CHAPTER 8:

Lawfulness Leads to Peaceful Prosperity

PREFACE

Funded by a mysterious web of international resources, in 2018 and 2019, caravans of thousands of Central American migrants boldly traversed hundreds of miles on foot in order to cross the US southern border.[127] Mostly men, along with some women and children from El Salvador, Honduras, and Guatemala, filled these controversial caravans.[128] These unprecedented attempts to enter America have added gasoline to an already fiery debate.

The tragic stories of Central American migrants elicit compassion from Americans on both sides of the aisle. However, MSM has severely limited the possibility of any commonsense bipartisan proposal by categorizing as bigoted and racist any who oppose an open-border ideology.[129] An open-border debate is not new; similar arguments have been in place since before the dawn of America. What has changed, however, is its wholesale adoption by the Left.

Historically, Democrats have opposed illegal immigration. As recently as 2006, many Democrats fought tooth-and-nail against illegal immigration due to concerns surrounding low-wage competition to their union base.[130] However, at present, virtually all Democratic leaders embrace open borders and amnesty.[131]

What changed? In one word: *demographics*. For the Left, the debate is no longer about public policy implications; it is about politics. The platform is about giving future Democratic voters the right to vote. With an estimated 22 million people residing within our borders illegally, the Left sees their path to power.[132] Consequently, the script has flipped from support for progressive "heroes" like Cesar Chavez, who persecuted illegal immigrants, to persecution of those who dare question the open-border ideology.[133] This shift in focus removes from the conversation the bipartisan sentiment of and collaboration for human flourishing for children in their home communities.

As the caravans attract the press, however, the untold story of the immigration debate is that of the families left behind.

The Northern Triangle

In 2001, at 18 years old, I served as a six-month missionary to Guatemala. Although I left Guatemala to return home, Guatemala never left me. The faces of the fatherless children I met live permanently in my heart. Eventually, in graduate school at Georgetown, I focused my thesis around homicide rates in Central America. Three nations in Central America—El Salvador, Guatemala, and Honduras—known as the "Northern Triangle," are much more violent than their neighboring countries.[134]

To conduct my research, I would take several trips to Guatemala, to study and witness the variables that made the region so violent. As I prepared to launch a new nonprofit, my visits were concentrated on the nation's most violent zones.[135] Although there was plenty of poverty, illiteracy, malnourishment, and income inequality, the most consistent variable plaguing the streets of Guatemala was fatherlessness.

As fathers are leaving Guatemala *en masse,* the region is experiencing record levels of violence. About 95% of murders remain unsolved and unprosecuted.[136] Economics play a major role in motivating fathers to flee. Although some families are lucky enough to see their fathers return home from the US after years of work, others never hear from their fathers again. Despite the increased income from remittances sent back by most fathers, the mass exodus of fathers has not improved the overall prospects for their families left behind.[137]

How this issue will shape the immigration debate is unknown, but one fact endures: an integrated family has a better chance at positive outcomes than a disintegrated family. The gaping holes left in the families in the Northern Triangle have forced many children to find their own way through the devastation.

Just as Jose Mendez did. Jose is a Guatemalan-turned-American citizen, and this is his story.

THE STORY OF **JOSE MENDEZ**

In 2010, a vision came to life when 97 at-risk Guatemalan boys attended a soccer camp with 19 mentors.[138] Champions in Action was created precisely for the purpose of connecting fatherless youth with life-changing mentors through soccer.[139]

The heroes of the Champions story are its mentors. One of these mentors has a story I know all too well. When I first met him, he was carrying an injured youth from his team up a steep incline to prevent him from having to walk in pain. That image, ingrained in my mind still today, is the perfect reflection of the life of Jose Mendez. Deeply impressed by that simple act of service, I sought to learn more about this young Guatemalan.

Jose eventually became the director of our mentorship program in Guatemala. He trained others to live with the selfless love he embodied for the kids from his team. His was a voice kids would listen to because he spoke with authority and legitimacy. Jose knew poverty and fatherlessness. Therefore, he could uniquely identify with the issues faced by these at-risk youths.

Many hundreds of volunteers have traveled to Guatemala to help in the one-week soccer camps. One of those volunteers is my youngest sister, Joanna. Through a series of events, Joanna and Jose became friends, but that soon turned into something more serious. Now, eight years later, Jose is my brother-in-law, and his two daughters are my nieces.

From Dependent to Independent

Jose was born in the late 1980s. He grew up in Guatemala with his mother and father, until his father left for America in the mid-'90s. Jose was not born into an ideal situation. Jose's mom, Rosa, from El Salvador, and his dad, Luis, from Guatemala, had met on a soccer field as teenagers. *Fútbol* turned into romance, which led to an unplanned pregnancy. Not at all happy with Rosa's actions, Jose's grandmother chastised her daughter and made her move back to El Salvador. Jose was born in El Salvador and was raised in his grandmother's home while Rosa worked.

However, the flames of romance between Rosa and Luis could not prevent Rosa from moving back to Guatemala—without baby Jose. Rosa's departure forced Jose's grandmother to take upon herself the unwanted duty of raising a child on her own. Little did she know she was raising a champion. Unfortunately, this situation led to a measure of neglect, and Jose became malnourished. Finally, Rosa and Luis learned of the baby's poor health and recognized their responsibility to save their child. Jose was then brought to Guatemala, where he gained strength under his mother's care.

Jose's situation seemed to be improving as he turned four years old. Jose's family lived in a colony called Galilea. At that time, it was a good place to live. His family attended church, and faith influenced their thinking. Luis had an established job, and Rosa took care of Jose and his newest siblings, Ana and Luisa. This brief window of security and peace would last only a few years. Soon Galilea became a red zone.[2, 140]

Even though the church was strong and the community was relatively safe, gangs and drug dealers began to infiltrate Galilea, and it became a major drug-trafficking hub. Galilea attracted dealers because it was connected to a number of other prominent drug colonies,

---

2 A red zone is a location identified within Guatemala as having relatively high levels of violence.

such as Paraiso, Alameda, and Limon. This area was a nice place to hide from rival gangs but also to monitor the individuals who would come in from the outside, whether cops or competing gangs.

The Departure to America

Luis had a stable job with Nissan for more than a decade, but he felt his income insufficient. He began to launch entrepreneurial ventures using credit cards to supply the initial capital. Over the course of several years, these businesses failed, and the Mendez family was burdened with a mountain of credit card debt—nearly 70,000 USD. For a middle-class family in Guatemala, this debt was roughly equivalent to 14 times their average annual earnings. The mounting debt began to squeeze Rosa and Luis.

Rosa began to pressure Luis to move to America. Luis initially resisted, agonizing over the decision. But when his mom died, Luis decided to follow his wife's urging. Luis already had a B-1 visa, which he would use to gain entry before overstaying his visa. With little communication or explanation to 14-year-old Jose, Luis packed his bags. Yet, the morning that Luis left, Jose knew his father was moving permanently.

Of the Mendez children, only Jose and his sister Raquel were old enough to comprehend the situation. Raquel was bothered by her dad's leaving and cried at his departure. Jose, though, was not close to his dad, and Jose did not really care if he left. To Jose, his father had checked out years ago, blaming his life issues on his wife and children. Not once did Jose hear from his dad the words "I love you." Jose would not speak to his father for more than six years.

Life for the Mendez family would change substantially upon Luis's departure. Awaiting remittances from Luis, Rosa began to work as a cosmetologist, and Jose would watch his sisters. Luis would send money back when he could, amounts varying based on the quality of his jobs. The vacillating income made it difficult for Rosa. Jose would find his mom in tears as she considered their desperate financial condition and overwhelming debt.

Due to Luis's departure, Jose's family could not keep up his private education fees. However, Jose valued his education and refused to quit. Jose tried to find jobs but there wasn't anything available for a 14-year-old, and he was forced to leave his school for a low-quality public school.[141]

Some of Jose's peers were involved in gangs, drugs, and alcohol. He feared the gangs and drug cartels, so he stayed as far away from them as possible. Despite his family's financial hardship, he refused to sell drugs. Many of Jose's friends would be killed within 5 to 10 years of their beginnings in gang life. For those who abstained, life was relatively safe. Gang members and drug dealers knew families by name and would avoid causing them unnecessary harm. This allowed Jose to pursue other dreams without deadly opposition.

A major shift occurred in Jose's life when he began to do track and field in high school. Instantly the sport became an overwhelming passion. His days were full; he trained mornings and evenings, attending school in between. When training, he could forget about all the problems in his neighborhood. He made new friends with his track and field teammates from different neighborhoods throughout Guatemala City. One of his teammates quickly became his best friend and welcomed Jose to his house to meet his family. This friendship would prove to become a source of tremendous blessing as Jose gained not only a friend but also a surrogate family. Given the challenges at home, Jose did not know what a healthy family looked like until he met this family. The parents became his spiritual father and mother and helped him to reconcile with much of the guilt he felt for his family's situation, filling the father gap many other young Guatemalans had, as well.

Soon, the family not only provided counsel but also recognized the material need of the Mendez family and offered Jose an opportunity to work. In a working environment with bosses who cared for his holistic wellbeing, Jose began to flourish. It was not long before Jose was able to make contributions to reduce the family debt through his income.

From Track to Ministry

As a gifted athlete, Jose was invited to continue his track and field career after high school. However, in the first semester of college, one transformational experience changed his life. One day, as Jose rode the bus home, he felt deeply convicted he needed to help fatherless youth. Too many of his friends were devastated by fatherlessness, the fathers of many having emigrated. Jose, also having lived this story, decided he needed to be like his surrogate spiritual parents to the fatherless youth on the streets.

Jose decided to go all-in to work full-time with at-risk youth. This change meant that Jose not only gave up his track career, but also the money earned through his job with his mentor. His mentors were supportive because they knew God had called him to this, but they also cried because they would miss seeing him on a daily basis. His mom struggled with it—Jose would be unable to provide any financial support for the family budget—but at the same time, she knew he was making a difference and morally supported him. Jose's work was with a Christian ministry in a neighboring red zone of Guatemala City called Alameda. The ministry could not financially support Jose—but miraculously, Jose began receiving donations from people he did not know, in support of his life and ministry.

Jose's decision changed the trajectory of his life. It would even cause Jose to reach out to his father to begin to reconcile their estranged relationship.

Champions in Action

Within one year of Jose's entrance into full-time ministry, his organization was offered 10 full-ride scholarships for boys from their program to attend a week-long Champions in Action soccer camp.[142] Jose would attend as the designated mentor. Not knowing what he was getting into, Jose had some apprehension, but he looked forward to a week with these fatherless kids, for whom he cared deeply.

Jose and his kids boarded a charter bus and drove five hours to a resort on the coast. Most of these kids, tattered and torn and with few belongings, hoped only that the week would not prove to be another disappointment in life. Jose resolved to make the week worth it for every one of them.

It was not long before the camp became a full-fledged training ground. Friendly competition enthralled his boys with the hope that they might win the camp championship. His team was the youngest, however, and ended up losing nearly every game. But through their tears and excitement, Jose would become intimately aware of each kid's story. Their lives had been wrecked by abandonment. They were desperate for guidance, for discipline, and for love. Jose was ready to lay his life down to ensure they got what they needed.

Of significant interest to his kids were the American volunteers who seemed to ooze love and compassion. It soon became apparent that their agenda was for each child to come to know the love of Christ. Through the course of the week, they would spend hours with these volunteers. But, more importantly, they found their surrogate father in Jose Mendez.

Every single boy from his team would make a faith decision that week, and every single one would confide his deepest and darkest secrets and fears to his newly adopted father figure. Jose's dream became a reality that week. He found what he was longing for and committed himself to doing it for as long as possible. Jose's work did not go unnoticed by the Champions in Action staff.

In the year that followed, Jose saw the power of the Champions in Action model and resolved to become a part of it full-time. Doors opened to allow Jose to become the first Director of Mentors for

Champions in Action. In addition to his 10 kids, he began to mentor the mentors. The role fit Jose like a glove.

The more he worked with mentors and youth, the more convinced he became that the epidemic of fatherlessness was at the heart of the violence. To that end, Jose became convinced that the departure of a father from the home, even for economic support, was a grave risk and likely not worth the sacrifice. Without some level of protection and wisdom, these young boys would fall into the age-old trap their fathers had. As he reflected upon the actions of his own father, Jose knew he had not forgiven his father for his absence and decided it was time to reconnect.

When Jose eventually tracked down and talked with his father, Luis, in 2012, he immediately felt bitterness rise to the surface. But Jose's bitterness arose not from his own pain but from sympathy for the fatherless youth he cared for. With a quick prayer and a dose of courage, Jose suppressed these feelings to tell his father that he forgave him and that it was his intention to stay in contact. Surprisingly, though detached from his family for more than six years, Luis did not display any significant emotion. Yet, Jose's act of forgiveness was less about Luis and more about Jose's ability to help his kids move beyond their pain of abandonment. According to Jose, only through God's power was this possible.

Changing Nations

Jose's new role as Director of Mentors exposed him to people he had never imagined meeting, like the ambassador of the United States to Guatemala, pastors of churches, presidents of organizations, and the sister of the author of this book. In fact, of all the important people Jose met, Joanna Jakubowski was the most fascinating. She was single and committed to her faith, and Jose and Joanna soon became an item.

Within two years, the two become one, and Joanna moved to

Guatemala. Their marriage strengthened Jose's resolve to serve the fatherless. The couple opened their home to kids in need. Not once did Jose think about living in America. His marriage was established in Guatemala, where he could continue to live the dream of serving the fatherless.

However, two years later, when they were expecting their first baby, Joanna's heart began to change. Living in Guatemala meant living away from her family support network. Joanna had soldiered on through many inconveniences, but being away from her immediate family felt unimaginable with a baby on the way. She soon began to appeal for a move. And Jose, for the first time, considered what it might look like to live in a different country.

As he pondered the move, he considered the thousands of others who gave their families away to move northward. This thought made him despise the idea of the "American Dream," which led him to resist a move entirely. However, the friction this stance created with his wife forced his hand. In 2013, Jose was awarded a five-year green card, which would lead to the move of the Mendez family from Guatemala to America.

Jose said goodbye to the land of his youth with nothing but gratitude. The love and sacrifice he experienced there had laid a foundation of hope for many formerly at-risk children. Now, with a new perspective and with a foundation of faith, these kids would choose life over death. Their ability to flourish in a difficult circumstance was made evident to them through Jose's life. Contrary to the example of his own father, Jose left his youth behind with fullness of heart.

Arrival in America was not easy. Going from director of a mentorship program to being a blue-collar worker challenged Jose. Aside from his family, Jose knew few people, and even fewer could empathize with his situation. Culture shock brought on some depression; he missed his Guatemalan family, his adopted youth, and his friends. But he overcame this trial with an abundance of faith. He built new relationships and leveraged technology to maintain contact with his Guatemalan family and friends.

The Formation of Political Thought

Throughout the transition, Jose began to minister to Latinos in Wood County. Through radio and outreach, Jose met many migrant workers and reached out to serve them. His unassuming character and meekness gave many of them the comfort to share with him their unique challenges and temptations. The more Jose served, the more he understood the severe challenges surrounding America's system of immigration. Although many of those who served with him were adamant about amnesty, Jose was adamant about *family*.

Coming from a story of fatherlessness, Jose believed that the best scenario for families from the Northern Triangle was for them to flourish in their home communities. Gandhi's famous maxim "Be the change that you want to see" has become Jose's rallying cry for his nation. He hopes someday to return to Guatemala and be part of that change.

Consequently, Jose views the immigration issue differently from most other Latinos. Jose believes in the creation of stronger borders to disincentivize the departure of fathers from their homes. He also believes in holistic reform, which eliminates family separation policies, increases the number of temporary visas, and gives the children of illegal immigrants a pathway to residency.

Jose did not become a citizen until 2017, which prevented him from voting in the '16 presidential election. Could he have participated, he would have voted for Donald Trump. Like other Latinos, he has concerns about the president's communication style. But the reckless rhetoric of the Left has awakened this new citizen to the principles of conservatism.

While the media would have you believe that the Left owns the Latino vote, Jose's story presents an opportunity to deliver a different narrative. Characterized by hard work, family values, and faith, Latinos are predisposed to many conservative ideals. But the aggressive rhetoric from the Right has helped the Left build a false meta-narrative of racism that many now believe to be true. Consequently, any support for border enforcement has been construed as racist or xenophobic. Yet, as Jose's story reveals, weak borders weaken families. The more conservatives make the immigration debate about family integration, the more likely they will be to win the votes of Latinos like Jose Mendez in swing counties.

CHAPTER 9:

A Blue Hammer with a Red Heart

PREFACE

There was a time it seemed that this chapter was not to be. When reviewing my outline with several close friends, one noted that the outline was missing one of the most important swing demographics in Ohio and in neighbor states Michigan and Pennsylvania: *the blue-collar vote*. The more I looked at the data in Wood County (referenced in Chapter 2), however, the more persuaded I became to include this chapter, and I am glad that I listened to my friend's advice.

Public polling has a powerful effect on voters' perceptions during campaigns. Research bears this out and has led to the creation of a whole lexicon of terms like *electoral preferences*, the *bandwagon effect*, and *horserace coverage*.[143] Billions of dollars have been poured into the polling industry by organizations, whether to profit from polling or to influence public opinion by encouraging or suppressing voter turnout. With 90% of DC journalists voting Democratic, it should be no surprise that leftist bias is par for the course.[144] Election 2016 seemed to build on this bias, observable through the media's widely publicized hate for Donald Trump.

On election night eve, a coronation ceremony awaited. The pollsters had spoken, and Hillary Clinton was bound to become America's 45th president. After a comprehensive compilation of polling from many sources, the *New York Times* famously compared "Mrs. Clinton's chances of losing to those of an NFL kicker missing a 37-yard field goal."[145] Throughout the campaign, conventional wisdom from both state and national pollsters demonstrated that Donald Trump never stood a chance.

Alliance Church Library
Oliver, B.C.

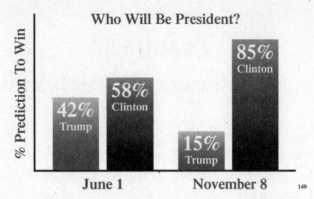

What followed the Monday coronation calisthenics was a Tuesday electoral miracle. Donald Trump's victory shattered the polls. Many have assessed and reassessed the events of November 9, 2016. One of the most comprehensive post-election polling analyses came from Nate Silver of FiveThirtyEight.com. Silver was unique among his polling peers, because he had given Trump a much higher probability of winning than his peers had—a measly 29% chance of winning.[146] In the midst of the endless criticism these pollsters faced, Silver declared that polling was not broken, but that conventional wisdom in polling was the root of the problem.

Unwilling or unable to change their approach, these same pollsters were back at it during the 2018 midterms in Ohio, predicting the unstoppable "Blue Wave." Yet, the midterm '18 results once again proved these pollsters dead wrong in the state of Ohio. October polling showed mostly Democrat-leaning numbers in almost every race.[147] In the end, Republicans won every statewide office, retained every congressional seat, and gained unprecedented majorities in the Ohio House and Senate.[148] Once again, the results ran contrary to the pollsters' overconfident predictions.

Naturally, swing-state voters have begun to question polling. The bias on display always seems to trend leftward. Are there any other underlying reasons for scientific polling to fail so terribly? This chapter will give a story to a population whose neglect has driven them into the shadows of opinion polling.

From Party of Labor to Party of Welfare

As noted in Chapter 2, the major swing in voting from between 2012 and 2016 in Wood County occurred in geographies filled with blue-collar workers. Many of these voters were left out of the discussion during the Obama presidency. Not qualifying on the Left's intersectionality slide rule, these voters were not worthy of the "change" Obama promised to America. The elites were enamored with a Europe-based one-world utopia that left the American worker out of the equation. As Hillary Clinton cast her elitist-European vision for America, identity politics were on full display: the white male, the benefactor of racism and privilege, ought to bear the blame and cost of social reengineering, which was not completed during the Obama administration.

Consequently, the American worker felt oppressed, attacked, and targeted. As lifelong Democratic voters with union ties, many American workers' allegiance had always been to the "party of labor." However, eight years of shrinking economic prospects shook their foundation and caused them to reconsider their party allegiance. *Enter Donald J. Trump.* Trump's message reached beyond the partisan barrier and into the hearts of these voters.

By now it is well known that many working-class white voters voted for Trump, but historically, this population has voted for Democrats. The near century-long marriage between Democrats and labor dates back to the New Deal era, when unions funded 10% of FDR's reelection bid in 1936.[149] What followed were decades of Democrats providing policy benefits in exchange for union campaign support, campaign dollars, and votes. Union families across America became established supporters of the Democratic Party, while Republican fat cats were their greatest enemy. This unbreakable alliance stuck through thick and thin as labor always opposed the Republicans, regardless of how popular they might be.

Pollsters anticipated the same trends in 2016, and polling data seemed to substantiate these claims. Had the prognosticators looked deeper, they would have seen a fissure beneath the surface, which reached deep into the soul of the blue-collar American worker. Philosophically, the American worker felt the Democratic Party's shift toward leftism. Many moved away from the Democratic Party out of a belief that it no longer supports the American worker but instead seeks to win votes by promising to give away things for free.[150] Why was this shift not recognizable?

The Untold Story

As I set out to meet with blue-collar millennials in Wood County who had flipped their votes, I began noticing a trend. I personally knew many older blue-collar voters who had made the switch and who were vocal about their decision. However, as I searched for millennials of this profile, I could not find one willing to take his or her story public. Nearly every one of them rejected the opportunity for an interview, even off the record. This trend finally awakened a realization that I previously did not see. Could it be that these voters were intentionally staying under the radar? Could it be that pollsters cannot account for this population due to their clandestine approach to their political leanings?

Knowing that I was on to something both significant and unusual, I decided to go to a source with knowledge and history in union life. His name is Jeff Bockbrader. Jeff served for more than 30 years in a union and rose to the top of his particular union segment, The Joint Apprenticeship and Training Committee (JATC).[151]

Union Man

Jeff Bockbrader was born and raised in Wood County. He spent a total of 35 years in the union, entering in 1983. He rose to and spent 13 years in union leadership. In order to join leadership as an agent, you are appointed by the state council. Similar to the advantages of a republican form of government versus a direct democracy, the representative process in union life was critical because it unchained the leader from the short-term passions of the members. At the same time, the representative was able to identify with the members, having been in their shoes. During Jeff's time in leadership, he grew close to the leadership of the JATC, and particularly the JATC president. Jeff's newfound friend was pivotal in bringing about reform to advance JATC interests into the 21st century. His leadership allowed for reform not only in recruitment and messaging but also in political engagement. According to Jeff, because of the president's leadership, the JATC is much more bipartisan than other union shops, as they have seen the benefit of working with both sides of the aisle.

Jeff's union was one of the first to endorse Republicans. Many other unions are much further behind and stuck in their old ways, using bullying tactics to persuade voters. The JATC received the greatest amount of pushback when endorsing Governor Kasich. A couple of other unions did this, but not many. The JATC was admirable in their willingness to look at a person rather than a party.

In addition to his union work, Jeff is unusual in that he owns a farm. This balance gave him a unique perspective from others in union trades, a perspective he hoped to apply in leadership. Although, Jeff grew up a Democrat, his well-rounded perspective as an attentive farmer enabled him to consider different viewpoints. Politics were left out of the day-to-day at the JATC, but during every presidential race, the conversation would find its way to the top. Contrary to other unions, the JATC would not pressure or force its members to vote in a given direction. Other unions would encourage members to "vote their paycheck," meaning to support the Democratic nominee.

Jeff, although not a millennial, was the perfect person to help me get a pulse on the Wood County blue-collar millennial vote. Having worked with thousands of millennials, Jeff, who has also worked with union men and women from other generations, has a unique perspective toward the millennials. According to Jeff, many millennials have a "blue hammer" and a "red heart."

It's not that Jeff thinks millennials are deceitful. But he believes their upbringing has taught them to appease the listener, telling them what they want to hear, even if they quietly think something else.

In Jeff's experience, millennials are more personal than previous generations but also more private. However, Jeff recognizes that blue-collar millennials are different from the stereotypical millennial, because they recognize the need to use their hands through labor. The kids that came out of the JATC were different from the norm. In spite of these differences, the relative-truth culture which all millennials were raised in has pushed this generation toward public demonstrations of political correctness, even if it contradicts what they know to be true. This clash of conscience and culture leads to a seemingly dualistic lifestyle, in which a millennial can virtue-signal in one venue while retaining a conflicting set of convictions in another. This is true especially of white, blue-collar males, whose social status among their peers may be damaged if their political views run counter to the established culture.

This quirk of millennials is why Jeff does not believe that polling can work with this base. They tell you what they think you want to hear. They're tough nuts to crack, because they will respond how they are *told* to respond, not with what they actually believe.

While pollsters were astonished by Trump's win in '16, the results didn't shock Jeff. Although not a Trump voter himself, Jeff could feel the energy and desire for change among the workforce. According to Jeff, "You would have to be blind not to see it, because there is no doubt that it exists. It's a well-known fact that many in the union supported Trump. If you listened to the people talking, the members, the youth, talked about wanting and needing change." Trump seemed attractive to them because he was not a politician. Trump's message mattered less to them than his persona. He was like a middle finger to the establishment, which drove them to support him. Jeff agrees with the overall sentiment, believing we need more people challenging the status quo of politics.

In Jeff's experience, millennials are even more private in conversation than any previous generation. Social media's blitz on privacy has provoked a guarded approach to relationships and conversations. With the potential ramifications of public exposure of one's beliefs on social media, the erosion of trust limits candor in political conversations with strangers, especially pollsters. A deep understanding requires deep trust.

At Jeff's encouragement, I continued looking for a millennial who would be willing to go on the record. According to Jeff, there are many out there, so it was simply a matter of time. He was right. Little did I know that throughout the duration of my research, my good friend and fellow millennial fit the bill perfectly and was willing to go on the record.

THE STORY OF **JEREMY HARPEL**

Jeremy Harpel was born and raised in Wood County into a hardworking American family. Growing up in Wood County, five miles from the eastern border, meant that life was slow-paced. As a boy, he hardly saw his dad during the week, because he worked second shift as a union semitruck mechanic. As a lower-middle-class union family, work was not op-tional. Neither was hunting or fishing to put food on the table. The time Jeremy and his older brother did spend with their father was often out in the wild; Jeremy had a hunting license at the age of nine.

Jeremy's life was typical of kids his age from eastern Wood County. These were boys raised on agriculture, hunting, fishing, and hard work. Nothing was handed to them. All of Jeremy's friends and their families understood the value of a dollar and lived by their ability to get a paycheck week to week. Many had worked on farms as children. Jeremy started bailing hay and straw at 13 and milking cows at 15. He would walk to work, two miles each way. Jeremy officially entered the workforce at 17 years old, working for a landscaping company.

Following graduation from Eastwood High School in 2004, Jeremy had several jobs. Like many of his friends, he looked at college, but the cost was too high. Being raised in a union house, Jeremy favored the trades, which provided immediate financial security without debt. From 2008 to 2014, Jeremy worked at a grain co-op (grain mill) called Luckey Farmers. This was a non-union shop of "farm boys or country bumpkins," Jeremy said. But all had the same work ethic and drive to trade sweat for cash.

Vote Your Paycheck

Jeremy's dad was a union man, and his family was going to be a union family—in their work ethic and in their voting. Growing up, Jeremy was taught that Democrats were the party of the worker and that he should vote accordingly. In '08, a lot of the younger blue-collar guys were excited about Obama because they seemed to relate to him in his youth. For Jeremy, Barack Obama represented hope and change in health care, in immigration, in foreign policy, and in trade. He came across as somebody who was going to bring change that the American worker could rally behind. The old guys were excited about the new candidate and were concerned about retirement health care because they didn't have it. They believed that medical care was deserved by those who *worked* their entire lives, as opposed to people who have depended on welfare their entire lives.

Jeremy's family and most of his blue-collar friends were strong Obama supporters in '08 and '12. However, their enthusiasm for Obama was tempered by the president's condemnation of gun rights. For these union workers, gun ownership was a way of life. As Obama's presidency continued, more things seemed to go awry. Shortly after Obama's comment of "they cling to their guns and religion," Jeremy and his colleagues felt like a lesser class, relative to the Chicago/LA/ NYC elite class of progressives. This was the moment when Jeremy began to take voting seriously.

For many people in eastern Wood County, it took approximately eight years for the disillusionment to fully set in. Relentless executive orders, political warfare, and the IRS scandal all began to nag at Jeremy's voting predispositions. For Jeremy and many of his friends, the attacks in Benghazi on September 11, 2012, were the nail in the coffin. Several friends with similar concerns didn't vote at all in '12, and Jeremy decided to vote for an independent.

Although tired of President Obama, Jeremy didn't feel right voting for Romney. Romney seemed out of touch, another elite with different networks. Gary Johnson seemed like a legitimate guy who could relate to farmers, ranchers, and workers. Jeremy didn't agree with all of Johnson's policies, but he felt Johnson related to working-class people. With a vote for Obama no longer an option, Johnson seemed the best alternative.

Enter DJT

Having worked in a plurality of blue-collar jobs, Jeremy, like his dad and brother, finally started working in a union job in 2014. Armed with new knowledge and antipathy toward President Obama, Jeremy fully expected to be in the minority. You work union, you vote Democrat. Much to his surprise, however, Jeremy found that many of the younger workers shared his frustration. Resolved to defy traditional union norms, they talked politics often and even questioned members of management with whom they disagreed. And once they started asking questions, they did not like the answers. Jeremy soon found a streak of independence among his younger fellow millennial laborers to vote conscience over paycheck.

From Jeremy's vantage point, pressure from union leadership was limited, because it was easier to get a new job than it used to be, and because people believed strongly in their autonomy and independent thinking. To Jeremy's surprise, this was no different from the Luckey Farmers' culture, where the employees were more focused on bettering themselves and their fellow workers than on sacrificing their individual success for managerial interests. A majority believed it was time to have somebody who could relate to them. Resentment brooded.

Perfectly timed, Donald J. Trump stepped onto the scene. No one even discussed Hillary Clinton, with the exception of maybe a few guys who whispered a word or two. According to Jeremy, the millennial generation from rural counties was more free-thinking than urban elites, because they were taught to think for themselves. Yet the elites seemed to ignore this population. According to Jeremy, the pollsters talked to the wrong millennials by talking with only urban millennials and not rural millennials. From Jeremy's vantage point, these elites didn't understand why people like him get up in the morning, why "we tie our boots and why we work." Jeremy was smack dab at the epicenter of this fissure between the Democratic elites and the blue-collar working class. The pollsters hadn't considered this. They assumed the labor vote was in the bag without having real conversations with people who were taught to question everything and think for themselves.

Due to Trump's stated policy platform and his running mate, Mike Pence, Jeremy and his colleagues felt they had a guy who could represent them well: both their paycheck and their values. Indeed, the blue hammer's heart turned red.

Looking Forward to 2020

As I concluded my interview with Jeremy, I decided to call an audible and ask him a machine-gun round of questions to get his immediate reaction. I was impressed by the strength of his convictions and his knowledge, so I decided to simply transcribe this part of the interview.[152]

Jonathan Jakubowski: Will the blue-collar American worker go with Trump?

Jeremy Harpel: Absolutely. Many are very, very happy with the job he has done. This group sees progress; they see steps taken for the security of the nation. We've seen jobs grow at an exponential rate, and unemployment is lower than ever before. Many times, people speak in opinions about politics, but today this class can talk in *facts* about what Trump has done. Owners are bringing their companies back to America, dealing roughly with China and Mexico. We deserve somebody to fight these battles, and Donald Trump is that guy.

JJ: Do they have any major concerns?

JH: They really like the non-PC nature of Donald Trump. He will say what he thinks regardless of where and who tries to influence him. The biggest complaint is Twitter-account usage, but at the same time, they love the way he is aggravating the "crazies."

JJ: Are rural blue-collar workers racist in their support for President Trump?

JH: These are political arguments of the Left to gain political points. The fact is that racism, as defined by the Left, is untrue. There is no way that we are more racist than the Jim Crow [era]. Everything is now race-baiting, but Trump confronts them by calling them fake news. These [blue-collar] millennials love this aspect of DJT.

JJ: Polling continues to show millennial opposition to Trump in 2020. What about blue-collar millennials?

JH: No poll will ever show how strong the millennial blue-collar vote is for Donald Trump. The Democratic elitists have no idea what it means to struggle. My car broke down and either I buy groceries or fix my car. That's real life where I am from. Thanks to the strength and the policies of Donald Trump, that life is getting better. These elitists like Sanders and Warren will show up at the big factories supported by Corporate America CEOs, but they avoid the true free-thinking American worker. For the guy putting in 40, 50, 60 hours per week, there is no connection to these Democratic elitists.

JJ: What do blue-collar workers think of welfare?

JH: We are compassionate people who will donate and assist the needy. But we have a problem with welfare as it stands today. Instead of being a hand *up*, it is now a hand*out*. The government has created a multigenerational culture of dependency. Much of the problem with Obamacare embodied this problem during the recession. Why am I spending my tax dollars on welfare and Medicaid for somebody else when I can't even afford a doctor's visit, and I am working more than 40 hours per week?

JJ: Did you know Trump was going to win in '16?

JH: I had a really good feeling about Trump winning. I try to keep a broad horizon by listening to multiple media outlets. Everybody I was talking to had conviction that Trump believed in "America First." We believe that it was time to put America First. We've been generous to other countries to the point of neglecting our own. Trump spoke his mind, he could not be bought, never was a politician, was unafraid of any enemy. When I started talking to my union friends—carpenters, mechanics—they were tired of the same elite families running the country for generations. They would ask, "When are we going to realize that it's time for somebody different?" They believed that Trump was the man for this.

Conclusion

The disparity in Jeff's and Jeremy's stories is revealing. In Jeff's story, the millennial blue-collar worker was guarded, whereas in

Jeremy's story the millennial blue-collar worker was publicly leading the charge. I don't believe this distinction cancels either of their stories. It actually strengthens the argument that the blue-collar millennial has a heart that turned red in 2016. Whether by false admission or omissions in polling, pollsters in Ohio have gotten it wrong. Not only did the hearts of American workers turn red in '16—those hearts appear to be beating red in '20.

PART 3:

A CRITIQUE OF MODERN METHODS OF CONSERVATIVE PERSUASION

CHAPTER 10:
PERSUADING THE SOUL

Seldom affirm, never deny, always distinguish.
—*St. Thomas Aquinas*

At the Constitutional Convention of 1787, 55 delegates from 12 states came prepared to defend each state's unique interests. The fact that these delegates, distinct in opinion, were able to achieve a compromise was "little short of a miracle," according to President and Deputy of the Convention George Washington.[153] One decade earlier, the fragile republic had experienced a breakthrough on Independence Day. Since then it had defeated the redcoats while narrowly avoiding dissolution and failure. As the hot summer months of '87 rolled in, many looked on skeptically at the compromises made to hammer out the proposed Constitution. It was at this moment Benjamin Franklin, the Convention's aged sage, handed his notes to fellow Pennsylvanian James Wilson to read a carefully drafted speech:

> "It therefore astonishes me, Sir, to find this system approaching so near to perfection as it does; and I think it will astonish our enemies, who are waiting with confidence to hear that our councils are confounded like those of the Builders of Babel; and that our States are on the point of separation, only to meet hereafter for the purpose of cutting one another's throats. Thus I consent, Sir, to this Constitution because I expect no better, and because I am not sure, that it is not the best.... On the whole, Sir, I can not help expressing a wish that every member of the Convention

who may still have objections to it, would with me, on this occasion doubt a little of his own infallibility, and to make manifest our unanimity, put his name to this instrument."[154]

Of the 55 delegates who participated, 39 signed the document. They hailed from 12 states, with only Rhode Island refusing to participate.[3] Franklin's words might not have motivated unanimity among the delegates immediately, but his continued pursuit of unity remains one of the principal factors leading to the breakthrough of an impasse.

Today, America once again finds itself at an impasse. I have demonstrated throughout this book how the Left has traded the higher ground of classical liberalism for the swamplands of the far-left. However, the aim of this chapter is to assess the weaknesses of conservatives and what has prevented them from reaching the millennial soul.

The Exhausted Majority: Bellwether Blues

Americans today are severely divided, with each side questioning the other's motives and character. We are unwilling to listen to diverse perspectives. At home, polarization is souring personal relationships, ruining Thanksgiving dinners, and driving families apart.[155] A majority of Americans, who have been called the "Exhausted Majority," are fed up by America's polarization. Stuck in a depressing state of cynicism and mistrust toward American politics, these voters are fast losing hope. This is the group that motivates the title of this book. These are the "bellwether" voters who have the "blues."

Yet research shows there is still hope. Notwithstanding their bellwether blues, these voters believe we have more in common than that which divides us: our belief in freedom, equality, patriotism, and the pursuit of the American dream.[156] They want to move past our differ-

---

3 Rhode Island refused to participate due to concerns related to centralized government taking power from state government.

ences. They are likely to align their ideology with friends who persuade, not with enemies who divide. In fact, the best prescription for the bellwether blues is good old-fashioned kindness, conviction, and inspiration.

The Exhausted Majority is made up of mostly politically disengaged independents. As noted in chapters 1 and 2, millennials are mostly independent. In Wood County, of the approximately 29,000 registered millennial voters, 70% are registered as independent.[157] This trend is unlikely to change anytime soon, as polarization drives millennial voters away from traditional party boundaries. The importance of this voting bloc cannot be overstated. Many of these voters classify the swing vote that decides the presidential election every four years. With the Left abandoning the principles of classical liberalism, and conservatives being unable to effectively communicate the principles of the Republican Party platform, the independent mind does not know where to turn.

To reach the Exhausted Majority, conservatives must change their methods of persuasion. How can we emulate the change that occurred in the lives of the stories shared in this book? In Swing County America, thousands of millennials' votes hang in the balance. Everything begins and ends with meaningful relationships—but how does one get there with a skeptic?

Persuade rather than debate.

Unify rather than divide.

Simplify rather than complicate.

This chapter unpacks each of these methods while critiquing the traditional conservative approach.

Persuade vs. Debate

When millennials make political judgments, their conclusions are often the result of years of thinking that have followed environmental influences created by their peers, professors, parents, and culture. The good news for conservatives is that the current mindset is only a pre-disposition; it is not a fixed destiny.[158] The bad news for conservatives is that their current approach to messaging is not working. Time after time, most conservative leaders resort to provocations of fear, esoteric economic explanations, or cold rebuttals absent of empathy.

The conventional prediction that voters grow more conservative after turning 30 years old is now in doubt. My former college football strength coach at BGSU continuously applied Einstein's quote, "The definition of insanity is doing the same thing over and over again and expecting different results." Millennials differ from previous genera-tions. The advent of technology, the relatively limited exposure to war, the rise of the Left in culture and education, the unparalleled prosper-ity and comforts of the 21st century, the decline in the centrality of faith—all have played a major role in shaping the millennial psyche. These formidable forces helped to create the prevailing left-of-cen-ter majority predisposition, assumed to be ironclad. Yet, contrary to leftist orthodoxy, human beings can overcome this predisposition—as they can any predisposition—when they are moved at the level of the soul.

Predisposition vs. Predetermination

It has been called the greatest ever meeting of minds.

In 1927, 29 of the world's brightest scientists traveled to Brussels, Belgium, to participate in the Solvay Conference.[159] More than half—17 of the 29—would become Nobel Prize winners.[160] Although lesser known today than Einstein or Curie, Niels Bohr was one of the most prominent scientists of his day. Bohr's recurring debates with Einstein during the Solvay Conference centered on the apparent contradiction between classical physics and quantum theory. His subsequent find-ings in quantum theory helped to establish our modern understanding of quantum mechanics.[161] Specifically, he was integral in developing the Copenhagen Interpretation, the baseline for quantum theory.[162]

I am sure you're asking, "What in the world does all of this have to do with persuasion?" Answer: quantum theory enabled science to mathematically explain free will, because nobody is predestined to think a certain way. Quantum mechanics provides the mathematical framework to prove that human thinking and choosing are real and measurable.[163] The power of leftist philosophy dating back to the *Communist Manifesto* is based upon the citizen as a victim.[164] Yet, contrary to the idea that we, including our state of mind, are nothing more than victims of our circumstances, neuroscience is proving that *our thinking* creates our state of mind.[165] Recent scientific breakthroughs reveal the power of human thinking on our condition. Science is proving that the brain does not rule the mind; the mind rules the brain. According to Dr. Caroline Leaf, "Our thoughts, imaginations, and choices can change the structure and function of our brains on every level: molecular, genetic, epigenetic, cellular, structural, neurochemical, electromagnetic, and even subatomic."[166]

Persuasion: How to Awaken the Soul

The implications of groundbreaking research on the mind are relevant not only in the philosophical realm of Leftism vs. Conservatism but also to the central thesis of this book. Predisposition is not predestination. Millennials are not hard-wired to vote exclusively to the left. Millennials have the ability to change their minds. This may seem like common sense, but many conservatives have all but given up on millennials. To make matters worse, conservatives have done a poor job of persuading them otherwise.

Many of us naturally believe that heated debate with sound logic will win over the listener. As research shows, the higher the emotions in the conversation, the more limited the logic.[167] Heated debate will not shake the foundation of the soul of the independently minded millennial.

Although times and technology have changed, people have largely remained the same. To impact somebody's perspective, you must have meaningful influence. In an age where relationships have become more transactional and less personal, people are searching for ways to create authentic relationships. For example, Dale Carnegie's classic *How to Win Friends and Influence People* sold more than 250,000 copies in 2010.[168] To relate to a millennial—perhaps a daughter or son, neighbor, or colleague—the answer is to dive deeper into relationship.

Deeper relationship is a longer, more difficult, less sexy road than throwing "truth grenades" and running away from the damage. But it is the road that will lead to the most meaningful change. Deeper and kinder conversation is an antithesis to today's campaign persuasion tactics filled with insults, snarky potshots, and ad hominem attacks. It is time to move from campaign persuasion into relational persuasion. A campaign is characterized as a battle between two opponents. Ideas are short-lived and superficial. Dialogue is non-existent; monologues play in stereo. None of these defining characteristics will work if you seek to persuade at the level of the soul.

According to Carnegie Associates, "The inherent relational value of influence has not changed (from the past). It is still the currency of inter-relational progress. Yet the plethora of communication media has made it possible to acquire dime-store versions. And you get what you pay for."[169] Millennials are accustomed to being inundated with bite-sized messages full of propaganda, vitriol, and self-centered messaging. Yours is the opportunity to stand apart, to make them better off, to invest in a relationship.

Conservatives need to think smaller. Rather than influencing the masses through a Facebook post, choose instead to influence one millennial who is in dire need of a mentor. Time as a fixed quantity limits the number of relationships that we can sustain. The more relationships we have, the less time we have to invest in one relationship. However, true influence requires that we become experts in a handful of relationships rather than a shallow contact of many relationships.

To use a modern-day axiom, rather than being a *Jack of many relationships*, it is more influential to be an *Ace of a few relationships*.

In the book *Crucial Conversations*, the authors highlight the fact that the primary predictor of success or failure in a project was whether the key stakeholders could thrive in crucial conversations.[170] Those who thrive in crucial conversations are able to remain calm under fire, preventing an emotional provocation from ruining their objectives in the conversation. In order to enter into highly emotional topics like politics, the most persuasive communicators understand that to move the souls of others, they must first inspect their own. These leaders begin these conversations with the right motives by premeditating and reducing the emotional response first within their own minds.[171] They are able to enter, maintain, and leave the conversation with three key questions governing their responses:[172]

What do I really want for myself?

What do I really want for others?

What do I really want for the relationship?

In reality, the more that you care about an issue, the less persuasive you are likely to be in a crucial conversation. Science shows that the moment you enter a conversation with someone who disagrees with you, immediately your raw instincts begin to take action. The hairs on the back of your neck stand up, your adrenal glands pump adrenaline into your veins, your brain diverts blood from nonessential activities to your arm and leg muscles, your vision narrows, and the higher-level-reasoning sections of your brain get less blood.[173] Your body prepares for the fight or flight *instinct*, and *reason* goes out the door. Without question, we have all had conversations where we later regretted what was said in the heat of the battle. Regret, however, can be prevented by confident humility.

The best approach is to share facts and stories while expressing an openness to learn from the experiences of others. (The next section will go into this in more detail.) A touch of humility and willingness to listen will go a long way toward the building of long-term trust. No matter how strong the leftist-monopoly on media and education, nothing is more persuasive than a trusted mentor and friend. The goal cannot be a political outcome; it must be long-term relational enrichment.

I repeat: the struggle for the millennial soul cannot be won through logical points delivered during a heated debate. As the stories in this book illustrate, millennials are less persuaded by oppositional debate than by story. America was largely constructed through logically written arguments filled with story and persuasion when national leaders turned to local papers to make their case. Take, for example, James Madison, Alexander Hamilton, and John Jay, who, using the pseudonym Publius, penned a series of 85 editorials to be read and debated across the country: *The Federalist Papers.*[174]

Where heated debate falls short, story and relationship hit the mark. Through applying the "Golden Rule," conservatives will rekindle the success of past eras, in which persuasion trumped power and violence. Millennials as a voting bloc will not be drawn to violence. Persuasion is best done by following the blueprint of the Civil Rights Movement. Martin Luther King, Jr.'s words and actions made a lasting impact on our nation and will forever be a part of our story as Americans. Rather than debating or fighting, MLK's aim was to persuade the soul, calling out Americans' dormant potential for reconciliation and peace. Thankfully, in 2020 and beyond, the opportunity to effectively deploy this strategy could not be better.

Unify vs. Divide

Millennials, more than any previous generation, have grown familiar with death. Morbid themes fill video games, the news, social media feeds, and the culture. Meanwhile, Americans spend a staggering 11 hours per day interacting with media, leaving them desperate for authentic relationships.[175]

To reverse this trend, it is imperative that authentic relationships point Millennials toward hope and meaning.[176] As already noted earlier, human beings are most influenced by relational equity.[177] As authentic relationships become less common, the need for them only grows. Yet authenticity in the digital age will not be found in skepticism or in disagreement. It will be found in *unity*.

Despite the prevalence of cultural skepticism toward anything and everything, most Americans still deeply desire unity and view it as both valuable and achievable. Unfortunately, the hyper-partisan state has created a monster. More now than ever, I hear conservatives suggesting that the only path to victory is through political warfare. Statements like "We have been too nice for too long" and "Win at all costs" reflect this brazen political landscape. Representatives are critiqued for being "too nice" or "too soft."

Every time I see a video of a crazy leftist assaulting a pro-life group on campus or a radical leftist legislator doxing teenage protestors at Planned Parenthood, my first instinct is to fight.[178] Yet, throughout the life of our constitutional republic, blood has been spilled by millions to ensure we could resolve matters through words, debate, and persuasion rather than through death, peril, and the sword. Unquestionably the option exists to form paramilitary groups like the alt-right or Antifa, but this response is not only short-sighted: it is un-American.

The seven stories in this book have shown people who may have been partially motivated by their enemies but who have been unquestionably influenced by their friends. In 2008, research was published in the *British Medical Journal* entitled "Dynamic Spread of Happiness in a Large Social Network." The study followed 4,739 people from 1983 to 2003 who were assessed for their happiness every few years, using a standard measure. The research found that human happiness increased by 9% with the addition of a happy friend.[179] If we can add 9% of happiness to somebody's life through friendship, I would argue that we have increased our influence by *at least* 9%.

When conservatives destroy bridges of friendship due to political philosophy, they lose pathways of influence. Although attacking an acquaintance might feel justified in the Wild West of social media, lasting impact comes from a thoughtful response that leaves out personal attacks. Personal attacks spill into the "real world," making recovery of lost relationships increasingly difficult. The relational damage has reached a global scale leading Pope Francis to call all Catholics to give up trolling for Lent, "we live in an atmosphere polluted by too much violence, too many offensive and harmful words, which are amplified by the internet."[180] Rather than ranting on Facebook, my encouragement is to invest in meaningful relationships. This might mean reaching out to a social media enemy, a wayward grandchild, or an unknown neighbor. What follows are five practical tips to help foster unity to build relationship.

Unify—How to Awaken the Soul

1. **Know Why:** Before persuading the soul of somebody else, it is imperative that you first have a soul-deep knowledge of yourself. You must understand why you believe in conservative principles and why they are the most persuasive, compassionate, and human-elevating convictions in the world. On my personal journey to embrace conservative principles, one of my favorite questions for people of influence was "What are your top three books?" I found this question enlightening and have benefited significantly from others' recommendations.

   Exercise: Read my top three: Arthur Brooks, *The Conservative Heart*; Henry Hazlitt, *Economics in One Lesson*; and Os Guinness, *Last Call for Liberty*.

2. **Listen Well:** The best listeners in our lives are often the people we depend on the most. Simply think about the best listener in your life. Now ask yourself, "Is this person somebody I trust?" Sometimes the best argument is made without words. Instead,

it is made by displaying genuine interest in the person you are seeking to persuade. If you are going to reach the soul, *trust* is the must-have currency; earn it by listening.

Exercise: Set up a coffee meeting with a millennial and listen. Predetermine that you will value him or her by listening. At least 80% of the conversation should be spent listening.

3. **Ask the Right Questions:** Millennials value being heard. This is a generation trained to share their opinion. Asking questions generates dialogue, which reveals the purpose behind a belief. Deep conversation follows great questions. Some of the most intentional conversations I have had were derived out of a well-timed question.

Exercise: Take a moment to list five questions you can ask on demand. Five of the best political questions that have worked effectively for me are as follows:

1) What is socialism? Capitalism?
2) Do you value freedom and think America values it? Why?
3) What should be the role of government?
4) What would you hope for every American?
5) What do you like and dislike about Republicans?

4. **Share Persuasive Digital Resources:** We live in a digital age. The probability of an independent millennial reading one of your political book recommendations is about equal to the probability of a baby boomer creating a YouTube channel. The good news is that neither one is necessary to reach a millennial's soul. Instead, identify ready-to-go digital content that conveys conservative principles effectively. Not only will you show that you are "hip" enough to use technology—you are also much more likely to get him or her to take advantage of your recommendation.

Exercise: Identify five of the most persuasive conservative videos, no longer than five minutes each, and (after your meeting) send the millennial a text with a link to the video that most pertains to the conversation. My favorite resource for short, persuasive videos is PragerU.[181]

5. **Invest in the Relationship:** Stand strong in your convictions, seek to persuade, and ask the right questions—but if you're disagreed with, remain firm in your friendship. I know this is counter-intuitive to the efficient use of time, but even if your listener isn't immediately moved, value him or her anyway. Walter Winchell once said, "A real friend is one who walks in when the rest of the world walks out."[182] In a world full of vitriol and skepticism, the best medicine to a hurting soul is a true friend. Millennials, as much as any other generation, need real friends who are present. After all, as witnessed throughout this book, the evolution of transformation of the soul is most likely to be a slow process. While Facebook friends or Twitter followers are a shallow exchange for meaningful relationship, true friendship is both meaningful and persuasive.

Exercise: Execute the **Listen Well** recommendation, and be prepared with a long-term plan of engagement. If the person questions your motives, speak honestly and let him or her know you are looking for a new friend to help you understand the way millennials think. Persist with humility.

Simplify vs. Complicate

Complicated. Confusing. Conflicting. These are commonly-held responses by millennials in response to conservatives' arguments. Conservatives would do well to simplify their message in the Information Age. During the past three decades, the quantity of digital information stored has doubled about every 2.5 years, reaching about 5 zettabytes in 2014, which is equivalent to 3,500 stacks of books reaching from the earth to the sun.[183] Can you say *overwhelming*?

The sheer amount of data and information has caused a paralysis of analysis, driving people to *emote* instead of *reason*. Regardless of the relational capital you have built, if the message is too complicated, your message will not reach the soul. Public speaking resources have pointed to the "power of three" in persuading audiences.[184] Is there a "message of three" that succinctly defines a conservative worldview? Before answering that question, let's define *conservatism* to discover the message.

Defining Conservatism

At the forefront of conservatives' battle for America's political soul is the battle within conservatism's own soul. In his book *The Infinite Game,* Simon Sinek describes how *leaders of infinite impact compete for transcendent values,* while *leaders of finite impact compete against the competition.*[185] Lasting impact in politics belongs to the political philosophy that transcends the times, the campaign, the technology, and the candidate. Conservatives should consider doing the most conservative thing possible: look to the past for guidance toward the future.

According to Larry Arnn of Hillsdale College,

"conservatism is the additional knowledge that things that have had a good reputation for a long time are more trustworthy than new things. This is especially true of *original* things. The very term *principle* refers to something that comes first; to change the principle of a thing is to change it into something else. Without the principle, the thing is lost. If American conservatism means anything, then, it means the things found at the beginning of America, when it became a nation."[186]

We can trace the roots of American conservatism to the document that outlines the vision statement for our nation, the Declaration of Independence:

"We hold these truths to be self-evident, that all men are created equal, that they are endowed by their Creator with certain unalienable Rights, that among these are Life, Liberty and the pursuit of Happiness.—That to secure these rights, Governments are instituted among Men, deriving their just powers from the consent of the governed."[187]

Within this powerful paragraph, the vision is cast for conservative philosophy.

Conservatism is the reflection that imperfect people are both endowed with unalienable rights and also must be the agents who secure those rights. In the words of James Madison in *Federalist,* no. 51, "If men were to angels, no government would be necessary. If angels were to govern men, neither external nor internal controls on government would be necessary."[188] Consequently, conservatism rejects the societal utopia leftism aspires to. Rather, it champions the principle of individual freedom, devolving the decision-making involved in one's pursuit of happiness to the individual, not to society. Government thus becomes a limited agency to protect the individual from external forces that might otherwise infringe on his or her freedom, as opposed to an agency securing happiness for the individual.

So, it should be no major surprise that conservatives hold to an "originalist" interpretation of the Constitution, whereas liberals believe in a "living Constitution." According to the *Heritage Guide to the Constitution*, "[Originalism] comports with the nature of a constitution, which binds and limits any one generation from ruling according to the passion of the times."[189] The deployment of this philosophy is not just limited to the judicial branch. As Utah Senator Mike Lee argues in his book *Our Lost Constitution*, every American citizen and all three branches of government are responsible for preserving the principles of the Constitution.[190]

Upon grasping the meaning of conservatism, the foundation was laid to simplify the message. Thanks to a newfound friend, I was able to find the message of three which could reach the soul.

Simplify: Awakening the Millennial Soul

Upon entering the bar of a Ritz hotel in Virginia in 2019, I found myself surprised by the height of Os Guinness. For whatever reason, I imagined this man of towering intellect to be short in stature. I was wrong. His 6'2" frame surprised me, but his warm smile was exactly what I had expected. Having read his books, I knew that this modern-day Alexis de Tocqueville, as he has been called, would be equally brilliant and kind. Like Tocqueville, a Frenchman who wrote *Democracy in America* in 1835, Dr. Guinness is a foreigner who has captured the essence of America as it is today.

Over the years, to help foster conversation with new acquaintances, I have often led with this ice breaker: "Amongst all of the people in the world, not being among your family and friends, name five people with whom you would most want to share a dinner." My own list includes Os Guinness. And in 2019, after months of perseverance, I was able to enjoy a three-hour dinner with this brilliant philosopher and kindhearted individual.

Dr. Guinness is an incredibly busy man, so his acceptance of my invitation was a tremendous blessing. Not only did he fully engage my questions—he was genuinely interested in the work I was doing. Our initial conversation covered a variety of topics across the board, including a bit of story sharing from both sides. However, it didn't take long before I started to ask a litany of questions I had written in preparation for this once-in-a-lifetime meeting. His answers reflected an incredible grasp of faith, history, philosophy, science, and politics. My furious notetaking simply could not keep up.

I quickly decided that rather than trying to keep up with the conversation while taking notes, I would take shorthand notes and pray that I could later decipher my illegible scribbles. Fortunately for mankind, my notetaking is not the only source for accessing the brilliance of Dr. Guinness, as he has authored dozens of books. Fortunately for me, he made a couple of statements that were so impactful that they have been etched into my mind. One of those statements was made after Dr. Guinness requested a summary of *this* book.

Rather than isolating the millennials from other generations, Dr. Guinness went into history and critiqued the idea of generationalism. Throughout history, movements and people groups were not divided by generations; they were divided into *ages*. An age is much longer than a generation. According to Dr. Guinness, the use of modern-day generational labels largely arose after World War II, as corporate America tried to increase consumer demand for products. While beneficial for revenues, this concept has created an unnecessary divide between age groups. Moreover, and having more implications for this book, generationalism does not reflect the common soul of humanity.

Whether a millennial or a silent or anything in between, all humans are moved at the level of the soul. Understanding what moves one's own soul helps one move a fellow man's soul. Dr. Guinness summed up this thought by noting that America of 1787 and America of 2020 require the same three ingredients for a flourishing society: faith, virtue, and freedom. This powerful combination, I contend, is the conservative message of three.

The Golden Triangle of Freedom

When I lived in Guatemala City at age 18, pure water was brought in from outside the city, and on a weekly basis, several water tanks supplying our house were filled. From time to time, unexpected water shortages occurred in Guatemala's water supply. Our house of 12 missionary students would immediately enter into a water-management protocol. The water from two tanks would be diverted into one tank for the primary purpose of supplying drinking water. This water diversion prevented us from showering, bathing, and washing clothing. I remember how much I dreaded the water shortages, due to the inconvenience. However, at the same time, my estimation of water's value was increased *ad infinitum* as I recognized how much ordinary life depends on it.

America, like the missionary house in Guatemala, has three reservoirs that have supplied its life-giving resources. If any of these reservoirs is deficient, the other two are at risk. Os Guinness used writings of the Founders of America to first identify and then to define these reservoirs as the "Golden Triangle of Freedom."[191] The Golden Triangle of Freedom consists of faith, freedom, and virtue. Each reservoir is independent of the others, but also interdependent *upon* the others. Today, these reservoirs are lacking the resources necessary to supply our beloved America. To restore each, we must seek to fill the reservoirs of freedom, faith, and family.[4] Let's look at each to understand how we can fill them.

Freedom

"It is seldom that liberty of any kind is lost all at once."
—*David Hume*

"There is not a more difficult subject for the understanding of men than to govern a large Empire upon a plan of liberty."
—*Edmund Burke*

"There is nothing more arduous than the apprenticeship of liberty." —*Alexis de Tocqueville*

One look at America today, and you might quickly question the statement that our freedom reservoir is empty. Americans today are the freest people in the world, in the sense that we are free from totalitarian government. This is defined as *freedom from*, or **negative**

---

4 Consistent with the notion that family is a proxy for virtue, I have replaced *virtue* with the word *family*.

freedom.[192] However, *freedom from* does not last long without *freedom for*, or **positive** *freedom*. Those who live a life of radical autonomy become chains unto themselves. Their freedom from totalitarian tyranny becomes a destructive force, as it leads them to become captives of their own desires. Addicted to vice, these individuals are unable to throw off the chains that shackle them. The freedom reservoir is therefore half full, and for those addicted to vice, it is half empty.

American freedom is unique in the world because it was born out of a vision for both negative and positive freedom. As I write this, I am sitting in a Parisian cafe on the Champs-Élysées, right next to the Arc de Triomphe. The Arc, originally envisioned by Napoleon Bonaparte in 1803, symbolizes the unity of France throughout the centuries. To capture this unity, this powerful global landmark must overlook incredible bloodshed, tyranny, and dissonance across multiple dictatorships and revolutions. Bonaparte dedicated the monument to military triumph; later, he left in exile. The Arc and its surrounding narrative stand in stark contrast to the Washington Monument, raised in honor of the man who freely gave away his power. This stark contrast arises largely from the different purposes of the American and the French revolutions.

In the late 18th century, two revolutions rocked the world. The American Revolution of 1776 created the longest-standing Constitution in the world today. The French Revolution of 1789 turned France into a perpetual bloody struggle for power and prompted an additional 17 revolutions. We would do well to look at 1776 rather than 1789 for our principles of freedom. Yet it appears that the principles of 1789—reason, enlightenment, and sexual freedom—reign in American culture today.

According to Os Guinness, freedom's origins matter, because freedom must have an origin story that leads to an end—a purpose—a "what for." American freedom looked upward; French freedom looked within.[193] In August of 1776, shortly after the Declaration of Independence was signed, Benjamin Franklin and Thomas Jefferson proposed the Great Seal of the United States to reflect the Exodus story of Israel being delivered from the Egyptian tyrant Pharaoh.[194] The prevailing thought fueling America's bold claim of independence centered on the benevolence of a Creator who called his people to covenantal freedom. So prominent was this thinking that many, like Samuel Langdon, used the comparison between Israel and America during the ratification debates for the Constitution.[195]

From the Mayflower Compact to the Declaration of Independence, American freedom has been characterized by a covenantal obligation similar to that of the Israelite people's covenant in the Torah. As Os Guinness writes,

> "People who covenant, whether in marriage or in nation building, make a morally informed and morally binding mutual pledge to each other that creates trust. The trust created by this mutual pledge is all-important because it replaces the need for force and regulation in relationships. It acts as the glue that binds as well as the oil that smooths."[196]

But to what are we covenanted? The answer is to "We the People." We are covenanted to each other. This is our *freedom for*. The French freedom of 1789 was exclusively centered on *freedom from*, empowering the individual to do as he pleased without restraint. This half-empty freedom led from one revolution to the next, ultimately culminating in 40,000 deaths by guillotine.[197] Radical autonomy turned into rebellion, which turned into tyranny. In contrast, the American freedom vindicated in 1776 is a holistic, selfless, duty-bound freedom. Although the principles were right, the founding generation was unable to extend them to all Americans. It would take a Civil War with hundreds of thousands of deaths to begin the process of freedom for black slaves. Right principles require upright people. As an American, my pledge of allegiance to the United States of America represents a commitment to advance the freedom of other Americans through self-restraint. As a former Navy SEAL, Jocko Willink noted, "Discipline is the path to freedom."[198] The covenantal vision of 1776 is the missing half of the equation in America today. This freedom to live for others is the *positive freedom* that will fill the reservoir, and this is defined by the other two reservoirs in the Golden Triangle of Freedom: virtue and faith.

Virtue (Family)

"Public Virtue cannot exist in a Nation without private, and public Virtue is the only Foundation of Republics." —John Adams [199]

"Only a virtuous people are capable of freedom. As nations become more corrupt and vicious, they have more need of masters." —Benjamin Franklin[200]

"To suppose that any form of government will secure liberty or happiness without any virtue in the people, is a chimerical idea." —James Madison[201]

"The diminution of public virtue is usually attended with that of public happiness, and the public liberty will not long survive the total extinction of morals." —Samuel Adams[202]

Today, if we look at America's fatherless children, rising crime, rising suicide rates, and drug proliferation, we look like a people on the brink of anarchy. The rule of law will demand an increase in governing authority to vanquish these threats, thereby decreasing freedom of the people. One recent example is the deployment of the National Guard after rioting erupted in Ferguson, Missouri, in 2014.[203]

The rise in anarchical protests with looting and rioting led to government-imposed curfews and restrictions. Simply put, a lack of virtue leads to a lack of freedom.

To reverse this trend, Americans must embrace covenantal freedom, built on the Golden Rule first exercised in the home. Parenting is the most important exercise of self-governance and the appropriate deployment of reason to help guide children. Anthropology, the study of human beings, defines humans as distinct from animals by their ability to exercise reason over instinct. Unless otherwise taught, children naturally revert to their basest instincts, which are naturally selfish. It is in the family where the child first learns to self-govern, if the parents are self-governing people. The result is a pluralistic society of self-governing people living lives of virtue, capable of advancing freedom.

"We the people" have come together to form a partnership nation on behalf of this freedom, which creates a just and peaceful community of free people. The future freedom of America depends on the virtue of its people. But virtue in the 21st century faces challenges unique to this generation. Although much of this book has lamented the political disunity separating the people, there is one present-day example of counter-productive *unity* between the Right and the Left that is destroying the lives of Americans with one swipe.

Tinder is a location-based social search mobile app, often used as a dating site, that allows users to like (swipe right) or dislike (swipe left) other users, and allows users to chat if both parties like each other.[204] Tinder has accelerated a culture of free sexual expression without commitment. According to Levi Lusko in his book *Swipe Right,* for the more than 100 million Americans on dating apps like Tinder, swiping right is increasingly the first step toward initiating no-strings-attached sexual encounters. Sex is being stripped by successive generations of any emotional or spiritual significance.[205]

In Tinder, the far-right culture of extreme capitalism with zero regulation and zero restraint finds itself in bed with the far-left culture of unbounded sexuality. This lethal combination spawns much of the anxiety and depression wrecking millions of millennials.[206] Rather than cultivating community, most modern-day apps are creating a façade of relationship, which accelerates hyper-individualization, leading to selfishness. And selfishness is exemplified by America's absent-father epidemic.

More than 1 in 4 American children live without a father in the home.[207] The results that follow are devastating:[208]

- Children living without a father in the home have a poverty rate of 47.6%, more than four times the rate of children living in a home with married parents.
- Individuals from father-absent homes are 279% more likely to carry guns and deal drugs than peers living with their fathers.
- Children in father-absent homes are twice as likely to suffer from obesity.
- Children in father-absent homes are more likely to experience behavioral issues.
- Children in father-absent homes are more likely to experience maltreatment and abuse.
- Children in father-absent homes are more likely to engage in delinquency.

Regardless of the form of government, for people incapable of self-government at the personal level, the inevitable outcome is tyranny by force. A morally irresponsible people cannot walk the narrow pathway toward human flourishing. They will fall into the ditches on either side of this path represented by the radically dangerous ideologies of the Far Right and the Far Left. Both ditches represent an increase in centralized power leading to suppression. We need not look any further than France of 1789, as the French revolution fostered radical autonomy, ultimately leading to the rise of a dictator.

Absent a miracle, America seems to be running headlong toward a destiny reflective of the French story of the 18th and 19th centuries. The fusion of radical autonomy without responsibility to unbounded sexuality, if left unrestrained, will result in a nuclear detonation capable of destroying America as we know it.

We need a miracle. Miracles can happen only in the realm of faith, which is the final reservoir in desperate need of being refilled. Restoration of the 1776 covenant means a countercultural embrace of virtue and selflessness, which can come only with another Great Awakening.

Faith

"Almighty Father—If it is your Holy Will that we should obtain a place and name among the nations of the earth, grant that we may be enabled to show our gratitude for your goodness by our endeavors to fear and obey you." —George Washington

"In time of prosperity fill our hearts with thankfulness; and in the day of trouble, suffer not our trust in You to fail." —Thomas Jefferson

"We have been the recipients of the choicest bounties of Heaven. We have been preserved, these many years, in peace and prosperity. We have grown in numbers, wealth and power, as no other nation has ever grown. But we have forgotten God. We have forgotten the gracious hand which preserved us in peace, and multiplied and enriched and strengthened us; and we have vainly imagined, in the deceitfulness of our hearts, that all these blessings were produced by some superior wisdom and virtue of our own. Intoxicated with unbroken success, we have become too self-sufficient to feel the necessity of redeeming and preserving grace, too proud to pray to the God that made us! It behooves us then,

*to humble ourselves before the offended Power, to confess our
national sins, and to pray for clemency and forgiveness."*
—Abraham Lincoln

*"Continue to guide and sustain us in the great unfinished tasks of
achieving peace, justice, and understanding among all men and
nations, and of ending misery and suffering wherever they exist."*
—John Fitzgerald Kennedy

*"Let us young and old join together as did the first Continental
Congress in the first step, in humble heartfelt prayer. Let us do
so for the love of God and His great goodness in search of His
guidance and the grace of repentance."* —Ronald Reagan

Many are the modern-day historians who critique America's faith
heritage and influence on government as nonexistent. Society today
accepts as fact that the Founding Fathers were deists who created a
wall of separation between church and state. Books such as *Our God-
less Constitution; The Founding Myth; Moral Minority: Our Skeptical Founding Fathers;* and countless others claim that our nation was
birthed with an Enlightenment mentality skeptical of any religious
influence on government. Although some of the contributions made
bring balance to the hagiographic status given to our Founders, much
of this thought is fueled by anti-Christian bigotry making outrageous
claims and ignoring the facts.

Among other factors of influence, the Christian faith was the
most influential force in the Founding era. Period. A study by Donald Lutz examined 15,000 pamphlets, articles, and books on political subjects published in the Founding era. He found that the Bible
was cited far more often than any other book, article, or pamphlet. In
fact, the Founders referenced the Bible more than all Enlightenment
authors combined.[209] In 1775, at least 9 of the 13 colonies had estab-

lished Christian churches.[210] Even following the passage of the First Amendment, six states retained state-established Christian churches.[211] Time and space do not allow me to add the dozens of national and state proclamations for prayer and fasting and the numerous letters written by the signers of the Declaration of Independence and the Constitution.

Lessons gained from the theocratic reign of terror of the Catholic church during medieval times would largely differentiate the American Founders of 1776 from the French of 1789. The Jacobins of France believed "that there would never be real freedom until the last king was strangled with the guts of the last priest."[212] Comparatively, the American Founders did not throw out the baby with the bathwater. They believed theocracy was wrong, but that true religion, and specifically the Christian religion, ought to be encouraged by the government because it was essential to liberty. In the words of George Washington, "Of all of the habits and dispositions leading to political prosperity, religion and morality are indispensable supports."[213]

In spite of the overwhelming evidence of the central role of faith, many secular historians point to an early-American history full of religious bigotry and persecution as proof of Christianity's incompatibility with freedom.[5] The argument is supported by several notable events in colonial times, such as the eviction of Roger Williams and Anne Hutchinson from Massachusetts, Puritan executions of four Quakers between 1659 and 1661, the Salem Witch Trials, Virginia's Anglican persecution of Baptists, and anti-Catholic sentiments throughout the colonies.[214] These black marks on America's record of religious freedom, left unchecked, would have prohibited the unity required for 1776 to happen. As the narrative goes, this

---

5 Conveniently, these historians point to violent events where dozens were murdered in America, as evidence of religious intolerance, while ignoring the hundreds of thousands murdered in other nations throughout the world at that time.

religious isolation and persecution was as vibrant in the 1770s as it was during the 1693 Salem Witch Trials. The problem with this argument is that it overlooks one of the most significant and unifying movements in history: the Great Awakening.

In addition to their disparate religious beliefs, the colonies were separated by differing economic interests, differing ethnicities, and a different vision of what constituted freedom. It was not until a 4'11" preacher stepped onto the scene in the 1730s that the minds of the colonists started to transform. Before George Washington, there was George Whitefield. Whitefield was America's first celebrity, traveling on horseback from Boston to Savannah, as more than 80% of Americans heard him speak live.[215] It is estimated that Whitefield preached more than 18,000 sermons throughout his nearly four decades of itinerant preaching.[216] It is said that when Whitefield entered a town, one could see clouds of dust surrounding the settlement, kicked up by the hooves of hundreds of horses bringing their owners as swiftly as possible.[217]

But, as with any movement, one man alone is not enough to change a generation. Thousands more would follow in Whitefield's footsteps: men such as David Brainerd, Samuel Davies, Theodore Frelinghuysen, and Gilbert Tennent would champion the message of the gospel.[218] These leaders from different denominational backgrounds taught a simple message: salvation was gained through a personal relationship with Jesus Christ instead of through an instituted church.[219] This message reached the soul of America, bringing unprecedented unity to the colonists and planting the seeds for independence. The Great Awakening forever changed America. If a colonist did not have to go through a priest to get access to salvation, he certainly would not need to go through a king to get access to his natural rights.

Faith was the unifying factor required to bring about America's independence, but more importantly, it was central to character reformation. In addition to the Founders' view on religious freedom, the Founders shared the conviction that absent faith, the Constitution could not stand.[220] President John Adams recognized the critical nature of faith and morality: "We have no government armed with power capable of contending with human passions unbridled by morality and religion. . . . Our constitution was made only for a moral and religious people. It is wholly inadequate to the government of any other."[221] In the Declaration of Independence, "the Laws of Nature and of Nature's God" was not a new phrase. This was largely derived from Sir William Blackstone and his book *Commentaries on the Law*, which was the most influential legal book in early America.[222] According to Blackstone, laws must be based on these two foundations: "[Upon] the law of nature and the law of revelation, depend all human laws; that is to say, no human laws should be suffered to contradict these."[223]

Contrary to nations like Israel at the time of Exodus or Muslim nations like Iran, America is not a nation covenanted "with God." These nations are theocracies, where belief in the God of the laws is a prerequisite for citizenship. Neither is America like France of 1789 or like North Korea today, which are covenanted "without God." These totalitarian states require a rejection of faith in God to abide by their law. Rather, America is a nation covenanted "under God." Citizens have the freedom to believe in any deity or none at all, but every citizen must abide by the law. As John Adams said, we are a "government of laws, and not men."[224] This form of government has enabled America to sustain a pluralistic society with diverse beliefs, convictions, and worldviews. The plurality of worldviews is a blessing. However, to achieve *e pluribus unum*—"out of many, one"— America must unify around and submit to the "Laws of Nature and of Nature's God." Regardless of one's theological stance, a third Great Awakening should be welcomed by Americans who desire unity. With every Awakening, America experienced increased freedom, drawing the people closer to the principles of the Declaration of Independence. If the diversity of denominational conviction in colonial America was not enough to prevent a first Great Awakening, perhaps the same is true in post-modern America. Only then will the "hearts of the children return to their fathers, and the hearts of the fathers to their children."[225] More and more, church leaders are calling for ecumenical prayer meetings, meetings of unity among faith leaders, community outreach, and a simplification of the message of hope. We are a nation of tremendous ethnic, religious, political, and geographic diversity. To sustain and advance this wonderful gift, our faith reservoir must be filled to the top.

Bringing It All Together

In the fierce competition for the millennial soul, conservatives will experience the *bellwether blues* if they sustain the status quo. It is time for conservatives to rethink their approach by playing the long game. The three reservoirs supplying America—faith, family, and freedom—are in dire need of being filled. As politics flows downstream of culture, culture flows downstream of faith, family, and freedom. The state of our union is far more predicated upon the strength of our families than on any presidential election. A self-governing people is the prerequisite for a flourishing republic. One's ability to self-govern his or her family leads to a lasting, multigenerational human flourishing. This truth must be defended against the endless attacks of secularism, which has led to the outcome of radically autonomous, hyper-individualized younger generations.

The conveyance of this truth does not require that we treat others as enemies. As stated by King Solomon, kind words are like honey—sweet to the soul and healthy for your body.[226] While I don't share Michelle Obama's political philosophies, I agree with her quote from the 2016 DNC convention, "When they go low, we go high." The road to relational influence, the high road, is often less traveled because it is more difficult. Are we willing to endure the insults, the mockery, the ignorance, the strength of opinion of our millennial neighbors? If the Golden Rule remains intact after all of that, you will have won the sacred relational trust necessary for influence. However, upon gaining that access, you must be prepared to deliver a persuasive message that reaches the soul. *Faith, family, and freedom*—this is the timeless message that will achieve just that.

CHAPTER 11:
The Road Less Traveled

I shall be telling this with a sigh
Somewhere ages and ages hence:
Two roads diverged in a wood, and I—
I took the one less traveled by,
And that has made all the difference.
—Robert Frost, The Road Not Taken

The rhetoric leading up to the 2018 midterm was heating up. Pundits on the left and right were attacking each other, many bemoaning the lack of civility on full display. Soon leaders on the left, including Eric Holder, Hillary Clinton, Maxine Waters, and Cory Booker, began to encourage violent resistance.[227] One student at BGSU, otherwise unengaged in the political scene, got sucked into the social media maelstrom. He soon became motivated by these statements and decided to act.

While at the Bowling Green Post Office, he took notice of several trays of thousands of slate cards with the faces of local Republican candidates. The worth of these trays, carrying thousands of pieces of first-class mail, was in the thousands of dollars. The student, reflecting upon his Facebook feed, decided it was time to act. Quickly he began to toss handfuls of slate cards into the nearest trash bin. This series of events led to one of the most meaningful exchanges I have ever had.

As a county chairman, I am responsible to ensure the successful delivery of slate cards to thousands of households. As noted, the production of these slate cards and the postage required to ship them cost thousands of dollars. One of our volunteers was at the post office preparing to send the slate cards. Due to the size of the crates containing them, he could not carry them into the room where he would pay the shipping costs, so he left them in the main hall as he paid, keeping the crates in his line of sight.

Upon reaching the counter, the volunteer noticed some movement out in the main hall. From a distance, the volunteer could see a young man messing with the trays. Visibly upset, the young man began to take out handfuls of slate cards and discard them into a locked trash receptacle. Not wanting to create a scene, the volunteer did not immediately intervene; he called me, asking for guidance. After a brief conversation, I encouraged the volunteer to confront the young man to save the slate cards that remained.

After the call, I hopped in my car, drove toward the post office, and called the county sheriff for guidance. The sheriff confirmed that such an act (tampering with mail, robbery) was punishable by law and should be stopped immediately. Furthermore, he was prepared to dispatch a unit upon my call.

When I arrived at the post office, 10 minutes later, I intentionally created a scene to ensure that the post office personnel would assist in apprehending the suspect if necessary. Thankfully, the volunteer had convinced the young man to stop what he was doing, but the discarded slate cards were still in question. I let the young man know that the sheriff was prepared to dispatch a unit upon my request. His face turned from aggravation into fear. It had become apparent he regretted his decision. Upon becoming aware of what was occurring, the post office personnel jumped into action. They asked if we wanted them to "elevate" the issue. My first inclination was to bring the full force of the law against him. But, now seeing his willingness to cooperate, I had an idea.

I politely thanked the post office personnel and let them know we would take care of it. I then asked the young man to join me outside for a conversation. He agreed and followed, and I began to describe his options. One option was to face the courts and to defend his criminal actions. The other option was to join me for lunch and a conversation. Thankfully, he chose the latter.

The following week, the young man, the volunteer, and I met in my office. For more than an hour, he described his story and the challenges he faced coming from a divorced family and living with depression. He was repentant, transparent, and humble. We then got to the crux of the matter about why he sought to destroy the slate cards. He described how social media had poisoned his mind toward Republicans, specifically toward President Trump. With liberal leaders like Maxine Waters, Eric Holder, and Hillary Clinton calling for war-like resistance, social media was ablaze with hatred.

Unaware of the divisions between local, state, and national party affiliations, the young man decided in that moment that he must #resist. The moment he was confronted with legal action was the moment he regretted his decision. After hearing his story, I knew the underpinning logic for his behavior was driven by emotion. However, by offering mercy instead of justice, I now had a listening ear and an open mind. I seized the moment to explain the "why" of conservatism, the foundation of America, and most importantly, the purpose of life. I gave him a couple of books, and we took a picture together and promised to follow up.

State of Conservatism

Absent any changes in conservative strategy, the *bellwether blues* will be passed from the Exhausted Majority to conservatives at large.

The young man who trashed the slate cards may not change his political leanings, but this experience has changed his entire perspective on politics, people, and faith. Many Facebook debates filled with excellent conservative logic turn into debate ping-pong with limited effect. Meanwhile, dissonance among conservatives, with their historic inability to define themselves, has opened the door for the Left to define the Right. This definition includes terms such as *racist, homophobic bigots*. This definition stuck with this young man until he could not resist confronting his sworn enemy.

The opportunity to influence the soul of a human being requires a balance of justice and mercy. Without the force of the law, it is unlikely that this young man would have experienced the fear that drove him to immediate repentance. However, without mercy, he would have been unlikely to listen long enough to change his heart. Mercifully—that is how the conservative ought to proceed, if desirous of a *conservative awakening of the millennial soul*.

Throughout the pages of this book, the logical appeals made by conservatives were unable to take root until the heart of the millennial was moved. Once the door was open, these swing voters connected with specific issues, which are part of the Republican Party platform: life, self-defense, freedom of religion, free enterprise, family values, the rule of law, and American exceptionalism. In every case, whether through friends, family, or candidates, the seed of one of these principles took root and catalyzed change in his or her voting pattern.

The 2020 election will be decided, in part, by the number of millennials who flip their votes between '16 and '20. However, the future votes of millennials in elections beyond '20 will only grow in importance and significance. While deep-seated change often requires long periods of time, there is no guarantee nor adequate predictor for how long transformation will take. As noted in the previous chapter, nobody is predisposed to think a certain way for the rest of his or her life. Yet it seems like today's identity-politics culture is warring to establish an inelastic generational chasm to prevent millennials from thinking like older generations. The chasm is built on the idea that the older and the younger have nothing in common and that nothing can be learned from each other. While there has always been some degree of intergenerational tension, technology has accentuated the tension to unmanageable levels. The age of information has created a post-modern fool's-gold version of wisdom that has elevated the hubris of the younger.

Under this tension, many aging Americans have withdrawn from the conversation, leaving 20- and 30-somethings to their own demise. To resolve it, individuals of true wisdom must breathe life into this chasm. The perseverance of a friend, family member, or neighbor has incredible power, even when it least feels so. Absent the courageous investment of older generations into the conversation, the wider the chasm, the more improbable the transformation.

As Os Guinness noted when we met, the concept of generation-alism was originally used to segment markets for the purposes of monetary gain. These generational differences, however, are of little benefit for the fostering of unity. The deft deployment of the tools recommended in the previous chapter will equip the conservative, but knowledge should not be confused with action. True moral courage, characteristic of the Greatest Generation, will lead to action, which is the only manner in which the chasm can be filled with meaning and unity. The *bellwether blues* will be felt by the conservative movement if this chasm goes unfilled.

As we conclude this book, I encourage a pivot in the conservative method and message to reach the millennial soul.

Cold Civil War

The challenge to act comes at a time of great adversity within America. According to Charles Kesler, America is engaged in a "Cold Civil War."[228] As Kesler explains, the Cold Civil War is not one of physical warfare but one of ideology, not of missiles and arms, but of words and ideas.[229] The danger of the present situation is that this Cold Civil War has led to an erosion of civility. Like the raging debates of the 1850s, the debates of today are testing our commitment to peace and goodwill in America.

The events of Charlottesville, Virginia, in August of 2017 symbolize the potential destination of our current debate. During that fateful day, physical violence was part and parcel of the protest and anti-protest raging between white supremacists and Antifa.[230] James Fields, from Lucas County, Ohio, which neighbors Wood County, drove his car into a crowd, killing one and injuring others.[231] His despicable actions, motivated by racism, put on full display the worst America has to offer. These actions, if perpetuated, will test the endurance of our republic as a Cold Civil War turns into a Hot one.

In the words of Lincoln in the Gettysburg Address:[232]

"Four score and seven years ago, our fathers brought forth upon this continent a new nation, conceived in liberty and dedicated to the proposition that all men are created equal. Now we are engaged in a great Civil War, testing whether that nation, or any nation so conceived and so dedicated can long endure."

Thus far, we have endured. Of all of the constitutions in the world, the US Constitution is the longest standing.[233] Since World War II, 729 constitutions have been written in the world, with the average constitution lasting less than 20 years.[234] Sometimes, in the midst of the political vitriol, we lose sight of the fact that our nation is exceptional among the nations of the world. Political problems are ever present throughout the world, and we must do everything possible to retain our constitutional framework to prevent violence from becoming the means to gain power.

Both sides have the opportunity to reframe the debate and regain civility. For conservatives, by redefining their methods of persuasion and by asserting a principles-first identity, they will fulfill their end of the bargain, as evinced by history. American conservatism served as the philosophical foundation for many of our nation's most important historical moments, which brought to life aspects of the unfulfilled vision of the Declaration. These include the founding of the Republican Party in 1854, the creation of the amendments to abolish slavery, the pursuit and achievement of women's suffrage, the fight against segregation, and the dissolution of the Soviet Union.

There is no better opportunity to deliver a distinguishing message. The Left, assuming that millennials are in sync with their values, has doubled down on its utopia of intersectionality. Take for example US Senator Gillibrand (NY) and her tweet on December 4, 2018: "Our future is: Female, Intersectional, Powered by our belief in one another. And we're just getting started."[235] Yet the seven stories from Wood County defy the logic of intersectionality, demonstrating how the stories of life moved those millennials to swing their voting preference. In every case, these millennials were moved by the stories of people who surrounded them. Whether family, neighbors, friends, or acquaintances, each was moved to the point of changing his or her vote. Neither skin color nor economic status was going to be the primary factor in determining their vote.

Most of the millennials interviewed for this book were not Trump enthusiasts or GOP die-hards. On the contrary, they flipped their vote from one that used to be persona-driven to one that became principle-driven. This solidifies their abandonment of identity politics, in favor of reason, persuasion, and truth. Their stories, centered in a bellwether county, indicate a potential trend among millennials where unquestioned allegiance to the Left's identity politics is becoming a thing of the past.

The American political future is in the hands of the party that can persuade both the soul and the mind of the millennial generation. The Left's abandonment of the center has opened up a window of opportunity for conservatives to make their case.[236]

Conclusion

There I stood, looking up at the 28-foot statue of Abraham Lincoln in the Lincoln Memorial in Washington, DC.[237] Those who stood in the memorial possessed a quiet reverence as they observed the perfectly designed features of America's first Republican president. The statue, although lifeless, seemed to breach the barriers of time to touch the living soul of each observer.

Although the intentions of the sculptors, who completed the memorial in time for the 1922 dedication, are unclear in some regard, there are unmistakable features about the man they sculpted.[238] Lincoln's left side reveals unwavering justice. With his left hand clenched and his left foot braced, Lincoln's statue brings to life the embodiment of a man who was resolved to see "justice for all." Lincoln's right side, however, reveals his side of boundless mercy. With his right hand extended and his right foot at ease, it brings to life his long-suffering kindness and empathy.

The more I reflected on this man, immortalized by the living, the more I yearned to embody what he lived and died for. His words, etched into the southern wall of the memorial, came to life that day in my soul:

It is for us the living, rather, to be dedicated here to the unfinished work which they who fought here have thus far so nobly advanced. It is rather for us to be here dedicated to the great task remaining before us—that from these honored dead we *take increased devotion* to that cause for which they gave the last full measure of devotion—that we here highly resolve that these dead shall not have died in vain—that this nation, under God, shall have a new birth of freedom—and that government of the people, by the people, for the people, shall not perish from the earth."[239]

Duty and sacrifice have always been part of America's story. This age is no different. The flourishing of America is predicated on the *increased devotion* of Americans to faith, family, and freedom. It might mean a gritty trek down the road less traveled, but should we persevere, it will lead to a conservative awakening of the millennial soul.

ENDNOTES

Preface

1   Online Etymology Dictionary. "Bellwether." https://www.etymonline.com/
word/bellwether. Visited on December 8, 2019.

Part 1: Setting the Stage

Chapter 1: The Millennial Dilemma

2   I'll capitalize *Left* and *Right* when broadly referring to these groups as thinking and acting as a single organism.

3   PragerU. "Ami Presents: Communist Manifesto or Democratic Party Platform?" February 16, 2018. https://www.prageru.com/video/ami-presents-commu-
nist-manifesto-or-democratic-party-platform/.

4   Taranto, James. "Divided America Stands—Then, and Now." *Wall Street
Journal.* June 30, 2017. https://www.wsj.com/articles/divided-america-stands-
then-and-now-1498851654. Accessed August 10, 2018.

5   Goodman, John C. "What is Classical Liberalism?" The Goodman Institute.
http://www.goodmaninstitute.org/how-we-think/what-is-classical-liberalism/.
Accessed August 22, 2018.

6   Wilt, Evan. *WORLD.* "Pro-life Democrats Becoming an Endangered Species."
January 22, 2018. https://world.wng.org/content/pro_life_democrats_becoming_
an_endangered_species. Accessed August 24, 2018.

7   Religious Freedom Restoration Act of 1993. Wikipedia. https://en.wikipedia.
org/wiki/Religious_Freedom_Restoration_Act#cite_note-2. Visited on August 24, 2018.

8   Bandler, Aaron. "Rubin: Why I Left the Left." The Daily Wire. February 11,
2017. https://www.dailywire.com/news/13389/rubin-why-i-left-left-aaron-bandler.
Accessed August 10, 2018.

9   Ibid.

10   Hook, Janet and Christi Parsons. "Obama Says Empathy Key to Court Pick." *LA Times*. May 2, 2009. http://articles.latimes.com/2009/may/02/nation/na-court-souter2. Accessed August 18, 2018.

11   Cooper, Brittney. "Intersectionality." *The Oxford Handbook of Feminist Theory*. August 2015. http://www.oxfordhandbooks.com/view/10.1093/oxford-hb/9780199328581.001.0001/oxfordhb-9780199328581-e-20. Accessed August 10, 2018.

12   Dershowitz, Alan M. "The Hard Right and Hard Left Pose Different Dangers." *The Wall Street Journal*. Written on September 10, 2017. https://www.wsj.com/articles/the-hard-right-and-hard-left-pose-different-dangers-1505073662. Accessed August 13, 2018.

13   Soave, Robby. "The University of California's Insane Speech Police." *The Daily Beast*. Updated on April 14, 2017. https://www.thedailybeast.com/the-university-of-californias-insane-speech-police. Accessed September 1, 2019.

14   Pierre, Dion J. "Demands for Segregated Housing at Williams College Are Not News." May 8, 2019. The National Review. https://www.nationalreview.com/2019/05/american-colleges-segregated-housing-graduation-ceremonies/. Accessed February 29, 2020.

15   Puzder, Andy. "The Market Will Set You Free". February 3, 2020. Prager University. https://www.prageru.com/video/the-market-will-set-you-free/. Accessed February 29, 2020.

16   Williamson, Kevin. "The Democrats Are the Socialist Party Again". June 20, 2019. The National Review. https://www.nationalreview.com/maga-zine/2019/07/08/the-democrats-are-the-socialist-party-again/. Accessed February 26, 2020.

17   Corn-Revere, Robert. "'I Will Defend to the Death Your Right to Say It.' But How?" American Bar Association. June 1, 2017. https://www.americanbar.org/groups/litigation/publications/litigation_journal/2016-17/summer/i_will_defend_the_death_your_right_say_it_how/. Accessed September 3, 2019.

18   Tobin, Jonathan S. "Liberals Sour on the First Amendment." July 3, 2018. https://www.nationalreview.com/2018/07/free-speech-liberals-turn-against/. Accessed February 29, 2020.

19   Pew Research Center. October 5, 2017. "The Partisan Divide on Political Values Grows Even Wider." http://assets.pewresearch.org/wp-content/uploads/sites/5/2017/10/05162647/10-05-2017-Political-landscape-release.pdf. Page 12.

20   Ibid.

21   Fry, Richard. The Pew Research Center. "Millennials projected to overtake Baby Boomers as America's largest generation." Written on March 1, 2018. http://www.pewresearch.org/fact-tank/2018/03/01/millennials-overtake-baby-boomers/. Accessed July 17, 2018.

22   Ibid.

23   Fry, Richard, Ruth Igielnik, and Eileen Patten. The Pew Research Center. "How Millennials today compare with their grandparents 50 years ago." March 16, 2018. http://www.pewresearch.org/fact-tank/2018/03/16/how-millennials-compare-with-their-grandparents/. Accessed July 31, 2018.

24   Ibid.

25   Ibid.

26   Raymond, Elora Lee, Jessica Dill, and Yongsung Lee. "Millennial First-Time Homebuyers and Location Choice." *Journal of Planning Education and Research*. Published October 25, 2018. https://journals.sagepub.com/doi/abs/10.1177/0739456X18807751?journalCode=jpea. Accessed September 4, 2019.

27   Pew Research Center. "The Generation Gap in American Politics." March 1, 2018. http://www.people-press.org/2018/03/01/1-generations-party-identification-midterm-voting-preferences-views-of-trump/. Accessed February 27, 2020.

28   Ibid.

29   Cilluffo, Anthony and Richard Fry. "An early look at the 2020 Electorate." Pew Research Center. January 30, 2019. https://www.pewsocialtrends.org/essay/an-early-look-at-the-2020-electorate/. Accessed September 4, 2019.

30   Fry, Richard. "Younger generations make up a majority of the electorate, but may not be a majority of voters this November." Written on June 14, 2018. http://www.pewresearch.org/fact-tank/2018/06/14/younger-generations-make-up-a-majority-of-the-electorate-but-may-not-be-a-majority-of-voters-this-november/. Accessed August 7, 2018.

31   Ibid.

32   Ibid.

33   Cilluffo, Anthony and Richard Fry. "Gen Z, Millennials and Gen X outvoted older generations in 2018 midterms." Pew Research Center. May 29, 2019. https://www.pewresearch.org/fact-tank/2019/05/29/gen-z-millennials-and-gen-x-outvoted-older-generations-in-2018-midterms/. Accessed September 4, 2019.

34   Ibid.

35   Stein, Joel. "Millennials: The Me Me Me Generation." *Time*. May 20, 2013. https://time.com/247/millennials-the-me-me-me-generation/. Accessed September 7, 2019.

36   Dorsey, Jason. "A New Take on Millennials." https://jasondorsey.com/blog/new-take-millennials/. Accessed September 5, 2019.

37   Ibid.

38   The Center for Generational Kinetics. "Marketing, Selling to, and Employing Millennials (aka Gen Y)." https://genhq.com/millennials-gen-y-generation-y-info-2/. Accessed September 7, 2019.

39   Ibid.

40   Honeycutt, Nathan, Radmila Prislin, Ryne Sherman, and Jean M. Twenge. "More Polarized but More Independent: Political Party Identification and Ideological Self-Categorization Among U.S. Adults, College Students, and Late Adolescents, 1970-2015." *Personality and Social Psychology Bulletin*. SAGE Journals. September 7, 2016. https://journals.sagepub.com/doi/full/10.1177/0146167216660058. Accessed September 7, 2019.

41   International Churchill Society. "Quotes Falsely Attributed to Winston Churchill."https://winstonchurchill.org/resources/quotes/quotes-falsely-attributed/. Visited on September 4, 2019.

42   Kirby, Jason. "Why businesspeople won't stop using that Gretzky quote." Maclean's. September 24, 2014. https://www.macleans.ca/economy/business/why-business-people-wont-stop-using-that-gretzky-quote/.

43   Hartig, Hannah and Stephanie Perry. "Millennial poll: Strong majority want a third political Party." Written on November 29, 2017. https://www.nbcnews.com/politics/politics-news/millennial-poll-strong-majority-want-third-political-party-n824526. Accessed August 12, 2018.

44   Berry, Jeffrey M., Jerry Goldman, and Kenneth Janda. "The Democratic Party, founded in 1828, is the world's oldest political party." *The Challenge of Democracy: American Government in Global Politics*. 2010 edition. Cengage Learning. Page 276.

45   Prokop, Andrew. "How Republicans went from the party of Lincoln to the party of Trump, in 13 maps." Vox. Written on November 10, 2016. https://www.vox.com/2016/7/20/12148750/republican-party-trump-lincoln. Accessed August 12, 2018.

46   Kahn, Chris. "Democrats lose ground with millennials." Reuters. Written on April 30, 2018. https://www.reuters.com/article/us-usa-election-millennials/exclusive-democrats-lose-ground-with-millennials-reuters-ipsos-poll-idUSKB-N1I10YH. Accessed August 5, 2018.

47   Walyus, Jeff. "Democrats are Leaving their Party in Droves. Conservatives Should Pay Attention." *The Daily Signal.* August 22, 2018. https://www.dailysignal.com/2018/08/22/former-democrats-are-leaving-their-party-in-droves-conservatives-should-pay-attention. Accessed August 25, 2018.

Chapter 2: A Swing County in a Swing State

48   Hunt, Albert R. "Win Ohio, and Win the White House." *New York Times.* October 21, 2012. https://www.nytimes.com/2012/10/22/us/22iht-letter22.html.

49   Barack Obama, October 30, 2008.

50   Archives.Gov. Distribution of Electoral Votes. https://www.archives.gov/federal-register/electoral-college/allocation.html. Accessed August 21, 2018.

51   National Popular Vote. "Two Thirds of Presidential Campaign is in Just Six States." https://www.nationalpopularvote.com/campaign-events-2016. Accessed August 21, 2018.

52   Silver, Nate. Five Thirty Eight. "The Odds of An Electoral College-Popular Vote Split Are Increasing." Written on October 31, 2016. https://fivethirtyeight.com/features/the-odds-of-an-electoral-college-popular-vote-split-are-increasing/. Accessed August 21, 2018.

53   United States Presidential Elections in Ohio. Wikipedia. https://en.wikipedia.org/wiki/United_States_presidential_elections_in_Ohio. Accessed August 21, 2018.

54   Archives.Gov. Distribution of Electoral Votes.

55   Encyclopaedia Britannica. "County Division of Government." https://www.britannica.com/topic/county. Accessed August 21, 2018.

56   Ibid.

57   2010 FIPS Codes for Counties and County Equivalent Entities. Census.gov. Retrieved July 5, 2018.

 https://www.census.gov/geo/reference/codes/cou.html. Accessed August 20, 2018.

58   Dent, David. Bush Obama America. http://www.bushobamaamerica.com/boacounties/. Accessed August 20, 2018.

59   Ibid.

60   Data USA. "Comparison Between Ohio and Wood County 2017." Deloitte. https://datausa.io/profile/geo/ohio/?compare=wood-county-oh. Accessed September 1, 2018.

61   NPR Staff. "Ohio County A Historic Predictor of State's Vote." NPR. September 29, 2012. https://www.npr.org/2012/09/29/162019588/ohio-county-a-historic-predictor-of-states-vote. Accessed August 25, 2018.

62   Comprehensive Annual Financial Report. Wood County, Ohio. Matthew Oestreich, Auditor. For The Year Ended December 31, 2018. https://www.co.wood.oh.us/auditor/pdfs/2019/2018%20Wood%20County%20Ohio%20CAFR.pdf. Accessed December 10, 2019.

63   DP-1 Profile of General Population and Housing Characteristics: 2010 Demographic Profile Data." United States Census Bureau. Retrieved 2015-12-27. https://factfinder.census.gov/faces/nav/jsf/pages/index.xhtml. Accessed September 8, 2019.

64   Interview with Terry Burton, Director of the Wood County Board of Elections. 2018 Voter Data as of 7/18/18.

65   Ibid.

66   Kolmar, Chris. "These are the Best Counties to Live in Ohio for 2018." Home Snacks. March 21, 2018. https://www.homesnacks.net/best-counties-in-ohio-1211916/. Accessed September 3, 2018.

67   U.S. Census Data. "Lucas County-Population Percentage Change 2010-2017." https://www.census.gov/quickfacts/fact/chart/lucascountyohio/PST120217#viewtop.

68   Reiter, Mark. "Lucas County Losing Population as Wood, Hancock, Fulton Grow." The Toledo Blade. March 23, 2017. http://www.toledoblade.com/local/2017/03/23/Lucas-County-losing-population-as-Wood-Hancock-Fulton-grow.html. Accessed September 3, 2018.

69   American Fact Finder. "Median Age by Sex-2012-2016." American Census Bureau. https://factfinder.census.gov/faces/tableservices/jsf/pages/productview.xhtml?src=CF. Accessed September 3, 2018.

70   Jones, Jeffrey M. "Americans' Identification as Independents Back Up in 2017." Gallup. January 8, 2018. https://news.gallup.com/poll/225056/americans-identification-independents-back-2017.aspx. Accessed August 29, 2018.

71   Wood County Board of Elections. Election Archives. https://www.co.wood.oh.us/boe/Election%20Archives.html. Accessed August 29, 2018.

72   Ibid. Author's note: Wood County added two precincts in '16 which are accounted for in the % breakdown.

73   2016 Election Results. "Ohio Results." *New York Times*. August 1, 2017. https://www.nytimes.com/elections/results/ohio. Accessed September 3, 2018.

74   Wikipedia Commons. File: Map of Wood County Ohio with Municipal and Township Labels. US Census, Ruhrfisch [CC BY-SA (http://creativecommons.org/licenses/by-sa/3.0/)] https://commons.wikimedia.org/wiki/File:Map_of_Wood_County_Ohio_With_Municipal_and_Township_Labels.PNG. Accessed September 7, 2018.

75   Office of Admissions. Bowling Green State University. "BGSU at a Glance." https://www.bgsu.edu/admissions/bgsu-at-a-glance.html. Accessed September 3, 2018.

76   While some residents live within the campus precincts and some students live in residential precincts, the data used is from Wood County precincts 10, 20, 30, 40, 50, 60, 70, 72, 90, and 100. The tables that follow are from Wood County Board of Elections, Election Archives.

77   Wood County Board of Elections, Election Archives.

78   The precincts with a >10% change include 50, 70, 100, 160, 170, 180, 200, 240, 270, 280, 300, 310, 340, 370, 371, 390, 400, 420, 430, 432, 440, 480, 500, 520, 540, 550, 570, 590, 600, 601, 610, 650, 652, 653, 662, 671, 770, 800, 810, 811, 830, 840, 870, 890, 892, 893, 900, 920, 930, 950, 960, 980, 999.

79   Wood County Board of Elections. Election Archives. The precincts included in this "blue wall" analysis for Lake Township, Northwood, and Rossford are 370, 371, 390, 400, 420, 430, 432, 810, 811, 830, 840, 870, 890, 892, 893.

80   TownCharts. "Lake township, Ohio Demographics Data." http://www.towncharts.com/Ohio/Demographics/Lake-township-OH-Demographics-data.html. Data USA. Deloitte. "Comparison Between Rossford and Northwood 2017." https://datausa.io/profile/geo/rossford-oh/?compare=northwood-oh. Accessed September 5, 2018.

Part 2: Stories of Principle

81   The lone exception is Jenna Cline, who, similar to the prototypical BGSU student, voted as a student and then moved after graduation.

82   The lone exception is Jose Mendez, who was not a citizen before 2017 and thus could not vote.

83   The quote's origin is unknown. American presidents riffing on the quote have attributed it to Tocqueville. Pitney, Jr., John J. "The Tocqueville Fraud." *The Weekly Standard*. November 12, 1995. https://www.washingtonexaminer.com/weekly-standard/the-tocqueville-fraud.

84   Vance, J.D. *Hillbilly Elegy*. Harper Publishers. June 28, 2016.

85   Moore, Karl. "Thinking and Emotions are Equals – More or Less." Forbes. https://www.forbes.com/sites/karlmoore/2017/06/26/for-millennials-thinking-and-emotions-are-equals-more-or-less. Accessed November 10, 2018.

86   Leonard, Alisa. "Millennial Priorities: The Rise of Emotional Intelligence." Levo Institute. February 17, 2017. https://www.levo.com/posts/millennial-priorities-the-rise-of-emotional-intelligence. Accessed November 10, 2018.

87   Ibid.

88   Ibid.

89   Gillman, Todd and Robert Garrett. 2018 Elections. October 26, 2018. https://www.dallasnews.com/news/2018-elections/2018/10/26/beto-orourke-tops-70-million-outpacing-cruz-2-1-texas-race-hits-100-million. Accessed November 10, 2018.

Chapter 3: The Poverty of Welfare and Its Destructive Effects on Fatherhood

90   National Fatherhood Initiative. "The Proof Is In: Father Absence Harms Children." https://www.fatherhood.org/father-absence-statistic?hsCtaTracking=-6013fa0e-dcde-4ce0-92da-afabf6c53493%7C7168b8ab-aeba-4e14-bb34-c9fc-0740b46e. Accessed December 15, 2019.

91   Pew Research Center. "Parenting in America." December 17, 2015. https://www.pewsocialtrends.org/2015/12/17/1-the-american-family-today/. Accessed December 15, 2019.

92   Jones, Jo and William D. Mosher. "Fathers' Involvement with Their Children: United States, 2006-2010." Division of Vital Statistics. December 20, 2013. https://www.cdc.gov/nchs/data/nhsr/nhsr071.pdf. Accessed October 7, 2018.

93   Tanner, Michael D. "The Poverty of Welfare." Cato Institute. 2003. Pages 20-21.

94   Keystone habits are those habits which are correlated to other habits, but are more important than other habits, because they spark chain reactions which help the other habits take hold. Charles Duhigg. "The Power of Habit." https://charlesduhigg.com/the-power-of-habit/. Accessed October 14, 2018.

95   Romans 12:2. https://www.biblegateway.com/passage/?search=Romans+12%3A2&version=NIV.

96   Warren, Shellie. "20 Most Common Reasons for Divorce." Marriage.com. Updated on January 21, 2020. https://www.marriage.com/advice/divorce/10-most-common-reasons-for-divorce/. Accessed October 14, 2018.

Chapter 4: The Unspoken American Genocide

97   Taranto, James. "Divided America Stands-Then, and Now." *Wall Street Journal.* June 30, 2017. https://www.wsj.com/articles/divided-america-stands-then-and-now-1498851654. Accessed August 25, 2018.

98   Number of Abortions – Abortion Counters. US Abortion Clock.org. www.
numberofabortions.com. Accessed December 11, 2019.

99   Vondracek, Christopher. "Planned Parenthood reports rise in government
funding, record number of abortions." *The Washington Times.* January 6, 2020.
https://www.washingtontimes.com/news/2020/jan/6/planned-parenthood-re-
ports-increase-in-government-/. Accessed March 2, 2020.

100   Green, Emma. "Science is Giving the Pro-Life Movement a Boost." *The
Atlantic.* January 18, 2018. https://www.theatlantic.com/politics/archive/2018/01/
pro-life-pro-science/549308/. Accessed December 11, 2019.

101   Ibid.

102   History.com Staff. "Harriet Tubman." 2009. https://www.history.com/topics/
black-history/harriet-tubman. Accessed August 26, 2018.

103   Alliance Defending Freedom. Planned Parenthood, the Whole Story. https://
www.adflegal.org/issues/sanctity-of-life/planned-parenthood-the-whole-story/
planned-parenthood-undercover-videos. Accessed September 16, 2018.

104   Pro Life Across America. "Know, Learn, & Share the FACTS about Life." https://
prolifeacrossamerica.org/baby-developmental-facts/. Accessed September 16, 2018.

105   Johnson, Ben. "Pro-life leader praises Donald Trump's 'exceptionally strong'
Supreme Court short list." Life Site News. May 19, 2016. https://www.lifesitenews.
com/news/pro-life-leaders-praise-donald-trumps-exceptionally-strong-supreme-
court-sh. Accessed September 16, 2018.

106   Save the Storks. "5 Myths Planned Parenthood Tells About Its Founder Margaret Sanger." Accessed December 14, 2019. https://savethestorks.com/2017/09/5-
myths-planned-parenthood-tells-founder-margaret-sanger/.

107   Riley, Jason. "Let's Talk About the Black Abortion Rate." *Wall Street Journal.*
July 10, 2018. https://www.wsj.com/articles/lets-talk-about-the-black-abortion-
rate-1531263697. Accessed September 17, 2018.

Chapter 5: A Women's Right to Defense

108   Brown, Anna, Juliana Menasce Horowitz, Ruth Igielnik, Baxter Oliphant,
and Kim Parker. The Pew Research Center. June 17, 2017, "America's Complex
Relationship with Guns. The Demographics of Gun Ownership." http://www.
pewsocialtrends.org/2017/06/22/the-demographics-of-gun-ownership/. Accessed
October 20, 2018.

109   National Coalition Against Domestic Violence. Statistics. https://ncadv.org/statistics. Accessed October 26, 2018.

110   Mahdawi, Arwa. "Weaponizing Women: How Feminism is Being Used to Sell Guns." *The Guardian.* May 17, 2018. https://www.theguardian.com/us-news/2018/may/17/tomi-lahren-nra-women-use-feminism-sell-guns. Accessed October 20, 2018.

111   Ibid.

112   Pavlich, Katie. "Gun Rights Are Women's Rights." Prager University. November 1, 2017. https://www.prageru.com/courses/political-science/gun-rights-are-womens-rights. Accessed October 20, 2018.

113   Crime Prevention Research Center. "New Study: 17.25 Million Concealed Handgun Permits, Biggest Increases for Women and Minorities". August 17, 2018. https://crimeresearch.org/2018/08/new-study-17-25-million-concealed-handgun-permits-biggest-increases-for-women-and-minorities/. Visited on February 8, 2020.

114   Perry, Timothy. "Beto O'Rourke says he expects Americans to surrender their guns." CBS News. October 25, 2019. https://www.cbsnews.com/news/beto-orourke-says-he-expects-americans-to-surrender-their-guns/. Accessed December 11, 2019.

115   Ohio Development Services Agency. "Ohio Export Internship Program." https://development.ohio.gov/bs/bs_oxip.htm. Accessed January 9, 2020.

Chapter 6: Faith Is Like Oxygen to Freedom

116   Metaxas, Eric. *If You Can Keep It.* Penguin Books. June 6, 2017.

117   Newport, Frank. Gallup Polling Matters. "Church Leaders and Declining Religious Service Attendance." September 7, 2018. https://news.gallup.com/opinion/polling-matters/242015/church-leaders-declining-religious-service-attendance.aspx. Accessed November 11, 2018.

118   Kramnick, Isaac and R. Laurence Moore. The Daily Beast. "Blame Evangelicals for the Decline in Christian Faith." June 16, 2018. https://www.thedailybeast.com/blame-evangelicals-for-the-decline-in-christian-faith. Accessed November 11, 2018.

119   Quoted in Michael Brown, *Saving a Sick America* (N.p.: Nelson Books, 2017), 182.

120   Unruh, Bob. "Attacks on Christians in U.S. Double in 3 Years." WND Exclusive. February 22, 2016. https://www.wnd.com/2016/02/attacks-on-christians-in-america-double-in-3-years/. Accessed November 13, 2018.

Chapter 7: Free Enterprise Is to Compassion as Socialism Is to Oppression

121 Sasse, Ben. *The Vanishing American Adult: Our Coming of Age Crisis.* St. Martin's Press. May 16, 2017.

122 The Economist. "The Resurgent Left. Millennial Socialism." February 14, 2019. https://www.economist.com/leaders/2019/02/14/millennial-socialism. Accessed December 15, 2019.

123 "The Congress, whenever two thirds of both Houses shall deem it necessary, shall propose Amendments to this Constitution, or, on the Application of the Legislatures of two thirds of the several States, shall call a Convention for proposing Amendments, which, in either Case, shall be valid to all Intents and Purposes, as Part of this Constitution, when ratified by the Legislatures of three fourths of the several States, or by Conventions in three fourths thereof, as the one or the other Mode of Ratification may be proposed by the Congress…" US Constitution. Article V.

124 Venezuela Investigative Unit. InSight Crime. March 1, 2019. https://www.insightcrime.org/news/analysis/armed-groups-propping-venezuelas-government/. Accessed December 15, 2019.

125 Pinkovskiy, Maxim and Xavier Sala-i-Martin. "Parametric Estimations of the World Distribution of Income." National Bureau of Economics. October 2009. http://www.nber.org/papers/w15433.pdf. Accessed September 30, 2018.

126 Kirchick, James. *LA Times.* August 2, 2017. http://www.latimes.com/opinion/op-ed/la-oe-kirchick-venezuela-pundits-20170802-story.html. Accessed October 5, 2018.

Chapter 8: Lawfulness Leads to Peaceful Prosperity

127 "Migrant Caravan: Mexican Officials Deny US Border Deal." BBC News. US & Canada. November 25, 2018. https://www.bbc.com/news/world-us-canada-46333119. Accessed November 25, 2018.

128 Ibid.

129 Jones, Reece. "Why Democrats should support open borders." *The Guardian.* February 16, 2018. https://www.theguardian.com/commentisfree/2018/feb/16/democrats-immigration-policy-open-borders-dreamers. Accessed December 23, 2019.

130 PragerU. "Illegal Immigration: It's About Power." October 29, 2018. https://www.prageru.com/videos/illegal-immigration-its-about-power. Accessed November 25, 2018.

131 Ibid.

132   Ibid.

133   Ibid.

134   Labrador, Rocio Cara and Danielle Renwick. "Central America's Violent Northern Triangle." Council on Foreign Relations. June 26, 2018. https://www.cfr.org/back-grounder/central-americas-violent-northern-triangle. Accessed November 20, 2018.

135   Jeter, Stephen and Jessica Mancari, Dave Schmidgall, Kate Schmidgall. "Coaching Futbol, Coaching Life." Bittersweet Creative Monthly. January 2015. https://bittersweetmonthly.com/stories/champions-in-action. Accessed November 25, 2018.

136   WOLA. "Why Central American Families are Fleeing Their Homes." Fact-sheet. January 2018. https://www.wola.org/wp-content/uploads/2018/01/Fami-lies-Fleeing-Factsheet.pdf. Accessed November 24, 2018.

137   Brazil, Noli and Jason Davis. "Disentangling Fathers' Absences from House-hold Remittances in International Migration: The Case of Educational Attainment in Guatemala." HHS Public Access. September 1, 2017. https://www.ncbi.nlm.nih.gov/pmc/articles/PMC4898477/. Accessed November 24, 2018.

138   The target attendance at each camp is 100 youth and 20 mentors. At several camps there have been absences, as in the first camp in November of 2010.

139   Champions in Action. www.championsinaction.org.

140   Jeter, Stephen, et al. "Coaching Futbol, Coaching Life."

141   In Guatemala, public schools are not free. Students are required to pay for their expenses, albeit at a much lower rate than at private schools.

142   According the Champions in Action model, the mentors are also the coaches for their team.

Chapter 9: A Blue Hammer with a Red Heart

143   Obermaier, M., Koch, T., & Baden, C. (2017). "Everybody Follows the Crowd? Effects of Opinion Polls and Past Election Results on Electoral Prefer-ences." Journal of Media Psychology: Theories, Methods, and Applications, 29(2), 69-80. http://dx.doi.org/10.1027/1864-1105/a000160. Accessed January 17, 2019; Lang, Kurt, Gladys Engel Lang. "The Impact of Polls on Public Opinion." The ANNALS of the American Academy of Political and Social Science. March 1, 1984. https://journals.sagepub.com/doi/10.1177/0002716284472001012. Accessed Janu-ary 17, 2019; Fitzgerald, Thomas. "Rethinking Public Opinion." The New Atlantis Journal. Summer 2008. https://www.thenewatlantis.com/publications/rethink-ing-public-opinion. Accessed January 17, 2019.

144   Joondeph, Brian. "Polls are just more Media Propaganda." Rasmussen Reports. September 6, 2018. http://www.rasmussenreports.com/public_content/political_commentary/commentary_by_brian_joondeph/polls_are_just_more_media_propaganda. Accessed January 17, 2019.

145   Katz, Josh. *The New York Times.* "Who Will Be President." November 8, 2016. https://www.nytimes.com/interactive/2016/upshot/presidential-polls-forecast. html?_r=0#other-forecasts. Accessed January 13, 2019.

146   Silver, Nate. FiveThirtyEight. "Why FiveThirtyEight Gave Trump a Better Chance Than Almost Anyone Else." November 11, 2016. https://fivethirtyeight. com/features/why-fivethirtyeight-gave-trump-a-better-chance-than-almost-anyone-else/. Accessed January 13, 2019.

147   Ohio 2018 October Elections Poll. Baldwin Wallace University Community Research Institute. October 8, 2018. https://www.bw.edu/Assets/stories/2018/2018-fall/cri-october_survey_report-final.pdf. Accessed January 20, 2019.

148   Ohio Election Results 2018. *The New York Times.* January 20, 2019. https://www.nytimes.com/interactive/2018/11/06/us/elections/results-ohio-elections.html. Accessed January 20, 2019.

149   Schlozman, Daniel. Scholars Strategy Network. "The Alliance of U.S. Labor Unions and the Democratic Party." October 24, 2013. https://scholars.org/brief/alliance-us-labor-unions-and-democratic-party. Accessed January 21, 2019.

150   Holloway, Carson. "The Great Revolt: Understanding Real Trump Voters." *Public Discourse.* September 30, 2018. https://www.thepublicdiscourse. com/2018/09/43720/. January 21, 2019.

151   Carpenters.org. https://www.carpenters.org/training_centers/oh/.

152   Interview with Jeremy Harpel. June 28, 2019.

Part 3: A Critique of Modern Methods of Conservative Persuasion

Chapter 10: Persuading the Soul

153   George Washington, Jared Sparks (1835). "The Writings of George Washington: pt. III. Private letters from the time Washington resigned his commission as commander-in-chief of the army to that of his inauguration as president of the United States: December 1783-April 1789. 1835," page 317. https://www.azquotes. com/quote/612762?ref=constitutional-convention.

154   Benjamin Franklin History. "Constitutional Convention." http://www.benja-min-franklin-history.org/constitutional-convention/

155   Dixon, Tim, Stephen Hawkins, Miriam Juan-Torres, and Tim Dixon. "Hidden Tribes: A Study of America's Polarized Landscape." More in Common. 2018. https://hiddentribes.us/pdf/hidden_tribes_report.pdf. Accessed May 10, 2019.

156   Ibid.

157   Wood County Board of Elections. Election Archives. https://www.co.wood.oh.us/boe/Election%20Archives.html. Accessed May 11, 2019.

158   Leaf, Caroline. *Switch on Your Brain*. Baker Books Publishing. 2003. Page 69.

159   Ashworth, Elizabeth. "Is this the greatest meeting of minds ever? Einstein and Curie among Seventeen Nobel Prize Winners at Historic Conference." Daily Mail UK. June 16, 2011. https://www.dailymail.co.uk/sciencetech/article-2002163/1927-Solvay-Conference-Electrons-Photons-Is-greatest-meeting-minds-ever.html. Accessed February 20, 2019.

160   Ibid.

161   Wikipedia. "Niels Bohr." https://en.wikipedia.org/wiki/Niels_Bohr. Accessed February 20, 2019.

162   Wimmel, Hermann (1992). Quantum Physics & Observed Reality: A Critical Interpretation of Quantum Mechanics. World Scientific. page 2. ISBN 978-981-02-1010-6.

163   Zyga, Lisa. "Quantum Theory May Explain Wishful Thinking." Medical Xpress. April 14, 2009. https://medicalxpress.com/news/2009-04-quantum-theory.html. Accessed February 21, 2019.

164   Engels, Friedrich and Karl Marx. "The Communist Manifesto Summary." SparkNotes. https://www.sparknotes.com/philosophy/communist/section2/. Accessed February 15, 2019.

165   Leaf, Caroline. *Switch on Your Brain*. Baker Books Publishing. 2003. Page 53.

166   Ibid. Page 68.

167   Grenny, Joseph, Ron McMillan, Kerry Patterson and Al Switzler. *Crucial Conversations—Tools for Talking When Stakes Are High*. McGraw Hill. 2012. Second Edition. Page 5.

168   Dale Carnegie and Associates. *How to Win Friends & Influence People in the Digital Age*. Simon and Schuster Paperbacks. 2011. Page xvii.

169   Ibid. Page xix.

170   *Crucial Conversations*. Page 12.

171 *Crucial Conversations*. Page 36.

172 Ibid.

173 *Crucial Conversations*, Page 5.

174 The Federalist Papers. Library of Congress. 1787-1788. https://www.loc.gov/rr/program/bib/ourdocs/federalist.html. Accessed December 15, 2018.

175 Fottrell, Quentin. "People Spend Most of their Waking Hours Staring at Screens." Market Watch. August 4, 2018. https://www.marketwatch.com/story/people-are-spending-most-of-their-waking-hours-staring-at-screens-2018-08-01. Accessed May 13, 2019.

176 Dale Carnegie and Associates. *How to Win Friends & Influence People in the Digital Age*. Simon and Schuster Paperbacks. 2011. Page xix.

177 Ibid.

178 See https://www.campusreform.org/?ID=12204 and https://www.newsweek.com/brian-sims-planned-parenthood-abortion-clinic-protesters-philadelphia-1418985.

179 Dale Carnegie and Associates. Pages 52-53.

180 Pullela, Philip and Hudson, Alexandra. "Pope Francis Calls On Catholics To Give Up Trolling For lent." Huffington Post. February 27, 2020. https://www.huffpost.com/entry/pope-francis-no-trolling-lent_n_5e56f774c5b66622ed765503. Accessed February 27, 2020.

181 PragerU. www.prageru.com

182 Winchell, Walter. Goodreads. https://www.goodreads.com/author/quotes/656830.Walter_Winchell. Accessed March 17, 2019.

183 Gillings, MR, M. Hilbert, DJ Kemp. (2016). "Information in the Biosphere: Biological and Digital Worlds." UC Davis. Retrieved from https://escholarship.org/uc/item/38f4b791. Accessed May 15, 2019.

184 Ginger Public Speaking. "Three is a Magic Number! How to Use the Power of Three in Public Speaking." April 13, 2015. https://www.gingerpublicspeaking.com/article/three-is-a-magic-number-how-to-use-the-power-of-three-in-public-speaking. Accessed May 15, 2019.

185 Sinek, Simon. *The Infinite Game*. Portfolio Publishers. June 4, 2019.

186 Arnn, Larry. "A More American Conservatism." *Imprimis*. December 2016. Volume 45, Number 12. https://imprimis.hillsdale.edu/a-more-american-conservatism/. Accessed December 16, 2018.

187   National Archives. Declaration of Independence: A Transcription. https://www.archives.gov/founding-docs/declaration-transcript. Accessed August 15, 2018.

188   James Madison. *Federalist Papers,* No. 51. February 8, 1788. Congress.gov Resources. https://www.congress.gov/resources/display/content/The+Federalist+-Papers#TheFederalistPapers-51. Accessed August 16, 2018.

189   Forte, David. "The Originalist Perspective." September 16, 2009. The Heritage Foundation. https://www.heritage.org/the-constitution/report/the-originalist-per-spective. Accessed December 26, 2018.

190   Lee, Mike. *Our Lost Constitution.* Sentinel Publishers. June 28, 2016.

191   Guinness, Os. *A Free People's Suicide: Sustainable Freedom and the American Future.* Intervarsity Press. 2012. https://www.rzim.org/read/just-thinking-maga-zine/the-origins-of-freedom. Accessed May 20, 2019.

192   Guinness, Os. *Last Call for Liberty.* InterVarsity Press. 2018. Page 86.

193   Guinness, 2012. Page 89.

194   Great Seal. Benjamin Franklin's Great Seal. https://greatseal.com/commit-tees/firstcomm/reverse.html. Accessed May 20, 2019.

195   Langdon, Samuel. "The Republic of the Israelites an Example to the Ameri-can States, by Samuel Langdon." Con Source. June 5, 1788. https://www.consource.org/document/the-republic-of-the-israelites-an-example-to-the-american-states-by-samuel-langdon-1788-6-5/. Accessed May 23, 2019.

196   Guinness, 2012. Page 89

197   Lynn, Michael. "Executions, The Guillotine and the French Revolution." The Ultimate History Project. http://ultimatehistoryproject.com/executions-the-guillo-tine-and-the-french-revolution.html. Accessed June 26, 2019.

198   Willink, Jocko. "Discipline = Freedom." Prager University. May 20, 2019. https://www.prageru.com/video/discipline-freedom/. Accessed May 21, 2019.

199   Founders Online. "From John Adams to Mercy Otis Warren, 16 April 1776." https://founders.archives.gov/documents/Adams/06-04-02-0044. Accessed May 23, 2019.

200   Gowdy, J. David. "Quotes on Liberty and Virtue." http://www.liberty1.org/virtue.htm. Accessed May 23, 2019.

201   Ibid.

202   Ibid.

203   Linshi, Jack and Victor Luckerson. "National Guard Presence to 'Significant-ly' Ramp Up Around Ferguson." November 25, 2014. http://time.com/3606063/ferguson-missouri-national-guard-deployment/. Accessed May 23, 2019.

204   Wikipedia. "Tinder (app)." https://en.wikipedia.org/wiki/Tinder_(app)#Concerns. Accessed May 23, 2019.

205   Lusko, Levi. *Swipe Right: The Life-and-Death Power of Sex and Romance.* Thomas Nelson Publishers. February 21, 2017. https://www.amazon.com/Swipe-Right-Life-Death-Romance/dp/1536616060. Accessed May 23, 2019.

206   Arnold, Daniel, Grayson Dimick, Lauren Linde, Hinnaneh Qazi, and Richard Scheffler. "The Anxious Generation: Causes and Consequences of Anxiety Disorder Among Young Americans." Berkeley Institute for the Future of Young Americans. July 2018. https://gspp.berkeley.edu/assets/uploads/page/Policy_Brief_Final_071618.pdf. Accessed May 26, 2019.

207   National Fatherhood Initiative. "The Proof Is In: Father Absence Harms Children." https://www.fatherhood.org/father-absence-statistic?hsCtaTracking=-6013fa0e-dcde-4ce0-92da-afabf6c53493%7C7168b8ab-aeba-4e14-bb34-c9fc-0740b46e. Accessed June 4, 2019.

208   Ibid.

209   Lutz, Donald. "The Relative Influence of European Writers on Late Eighteenth-Century American Political Thought." *American Political Science Review,* Vol. 78 (March 1984), pp. 189–197. https://www.jstor.org/stable/1961257?seq=1. Accessed May 30, 2019.

210   Hall, David. "Did America Have a Christian Founding?" The Heritage Foundation. June 7, 2011. https://www.heritage.org/political-process/report/did-america-have-christian-founding#_ftn20. Accessed May 30, 2019.

211   The Heritage Guide to The Constitution. Amendment 1, Establishment of Religion. 2017. https://www.heritage.org/constitution/amendments/1/essays/138/establishment-of-religion. Accessed May 30, 2019.

212   Guinness, Os. *Last Call for Liberty.* Intervarsity Press. 2018. Page 38.

213   Washington, George. "Washington's Farewell Address 1796." 1796. Yale Law School. http://avalon.law.yale.edu/18th_century/washing.asp. Accessed June 1, 2019.

214   Exhibitions Library of Congress. "Religion and the Founding of the American Republic." https://www.loc.gov/exhibits/religion/rel01-2.html. Accessed June 1, 2019.

215   Metaxas, Eric. *If You Can Keep It.* Penguin Books. June 6, 2017. Page 111.

216   The Digital Puritan. "George Whitefield." Accessed June 4, 2019. http://digitalpuritan.net/george-whitefield/.

217   Metaxas, Page 105.

218   History.com Editors. "Great Awakening." The History Channel. August 21, 2018. https://www.history.com/topics/british-history/great-awakening. Accessed June 4, 2019.

219   Ibid.

220   Hall, David. 2011.

221   Adams, John. *The Works of John Adams, Second President of the United States*. Edited by Charles Francis Adams. Boston: Little, Brown, and Co. 1854. Vol. IX, p. 229, October 11, 1798.

222   Morgan, Kerry. "The Laws of Nature and of Nature's God: The True Foundation of American Law." LONANG Institute. Accessed June 8, 2019. https://lonang.com/commentaries/conlaw/organizing/laws-of-nature-and-natures-god/.

223   Ibid.

224   John Adams Historical Society. "John Adams Quotes on Law and Politics." http://www.john-adams-heritage.com/quotes/. Accessed January 6, 2020.

225   Malachi 4:6.

226   Proverbs 16:24.

Chapter 11: The Road Less Traveled

227   Re, Gregg. "Eric Holder Rejects Michelle Obama's Call for Civility: 'When They Go Low, We Kick 'Em.'" Fox News. https://www.foxnews.com/politics/eric-holder-rejects-michelle-obamas-call-for-civility. Accessed February 24, 2019.

228   Kesler, Charles. "America's Cold Civil War." *Imprimis*. October 2018. Volume 47, Number 10. https://imprimis.hillsdale.edu/americas-cold-civil-war/. Accessed December 12, 2018.

229   Ibid.

230   Andone, Dakin and Laura Dolan. CNN. "Charlottesville Suspect Shared Posts Showing Car Driving into Protestors Before Attack." November 30, 2018. https://www.cnn.com/2018/11/30/us/charlottesville-james-fields-trial/index.html.

231   Ibid.

232   "The Gettysburg Address." Abraham Lincoln Online. November 19, 1863. http://www.abrahamlincolnonline.org/lincoln/speeches/gettysburg.htm. Accessed December 31, 2018.

233   Feulner, Edwin J., "The Key to a Long-Lasting Constitution." The Heritage Foundation. September 17, 2013. https://www.heritage.org/political-process/commentary/the-key-long-lasting-constitution. Accessed December 19, 2018.

234   Ibid.

235   Senator Kirsten Gillibrand. Twitter. December 4, 2018. https://twitter.com/SenGillibrand/status/1070106980298186753. Accessed December 10, 2018.

236   Pew Research Center. "The Partisan Divide on Political Values Grows Even Wider." October 2017.

237   Wikipedia. "Lincoln Memorial." https://en.wikipedia.org/wiki/Lincoln_Memorial#Statue. Accessed December 31, 2018.

238   Ibid.

239   "Gettysburg Address." Abraham Lincoln Online.

ACKNOWLEDGEMENTS

Never could I have predicted the twists and turns that came with writing a book. Among the most surprising was the fact that the Acknowledgements section would be this difficult to write. Yet there I sat, staring at the blinking cursor, overwhelmed by the amount of people I needed to thank for making this book possible. My greatest concern was that I would forget to mention somebody who made an investment in my life and in this book. So, I begin by thanking those whose names are not included below. The prayers, the encouragement, the editing, the strategy, and the myriad ways people made this possible are all meritorious of my greatest appreciation. Thank you.

Without the trust of Al and Kathy Caperna, Jeff Palmer, and CMC Group leadership, I would not have been able to write a book while leading SmartSolve. Your mentorship and leadership have played a major role in making me who I am today.

To Phil Weaver, your unwavering mentorship, prayer, and support are undeserving and they have marked my life. Greg Rogers, you were the initial inspiration behind addressing this topic and now your advocacy is an incredible blessing. To my prayer team, your continual prayers throughout this journey are immeasurable in their impact.

Gregg Emch and Victor Ten Brink, your legal counsel throughout the years has enabled me to complete projects I never thought possible. You are truly men worth following.

Special thanks to Michael Hamilton and the Good Comma Editing team. Your work on the manuscript raised the level of excellence of this book. Andy Symonds and the Ballast Books team, thank you for believing enough in this first-time author enough to publish this book.

From the very beginning, I knew that I faced an uphill battle when trying to market and sell my first book. Consequently, I assembled a team of amazingly gifted people to deliver beautiful photography, a best-in-class website, inspiring videos, and a polished brand. Joanna Mendez, the photography was beautiful and inspiring. Thanks for being there with me from the very first interview. Bevan Binder and Edzel Antiquina, you guys knocked it out of the park with the website and book cover. Jason Droll, you have kept the ship afloat with countless updates and changes to the website and blog. Thanks for being there with me from the very first interview. Vince Rocha, your amazing videography skills gave this book a lift before it was close to being published.

In a world where social media has the potential to be a nuisance, we wanted our social media strategy to reflect the heart of this book. Thank you Olivia Rogers for getting us started. Brant Kitchen, your contributions in the background with the newsletter and your promotional work have been tremendous. Joel and Sam Berry, you were the first to interview me on your podcast and now you are helping connect me to others nationwide. It has been a joy working with you.

Adam Josefczyk. Justin Powell, Aaron Baer, and Peter Range, you are friends and leaders whom I admire and respect. Your encouragement throughout has been a true gift. Brad Custis, before the book was ever written, you stated that you wanted to be the first to buy in bulk. Since our mission to Guatemala in 2001, you have never waivered as a friend; I pray that I reciprocate your loyalty. Chip Weiant, thank you for helping me with the prelude and thank you for your leadership in Ohio.

When we moved from Northern Virginia back to Wood County Ohio, many people thought that we had regressed. Quite the contrary. The richness of faith, family, and freedom in this county has taught me unforgettable lessons. Wood County might be small in population but it is large in its influence. I am indebted with gratitude to many people who make living in Wood County special.

For the leaders who endorsed this book, thank you for reading the manuscript and for believing in me and in the message of this book. I deeply appreciate that you were willing to take a chance on a first-time author. Your endorsement gives this book the credibility it could not otherwise obtain.

Alfonso, Arron, Douglas, Jenna, Jeremy, Jose, and Tiffany, your stories inspire others. Without your willingness to share your stories, this book would not exist. Thank you for being willing to take your story public.

Of all the people to help me choose a title, I would not have guessed Mark Rutkus. Mark is my brother-in-law who also happens to be a staunch Democrat who I respect greatly. Throughout all our conversations, the end is always family above everything else. After listening to my explanation, Mark was kind enough to recommend a title fitting for the frustrations that millennials face. Thank you!

To the Newlove family, being a part of a family of Democrats who embrace this conservative Republican should give us all hope. Family always trumps politics. To the Peters family, your prayers and support are force multipliers. I am thankful to be counted as family. To my extended Jakubowski family. Throughout life, we have shared in each others successes and failures. Your celebration of this book has meant the world to me. May we always be each others greatest supporters.

To my friend, mentor, and big brother, Shaun Alexander, thank you for a decade of wisdom. In spite of my shortcomings, you have been a faithful friend and continual advocate. I am a better man because of your example.

Finally, to Missy, Emelia, Judah, Samuel, and Levi, who sacrificed most to make this book possible. The hours spent writing the manuscript, doing interviews, launching the marketing plan, and traveling to give speeches were all hours that you gave up. Not only did you endure those many hours, you enthusiastically supported me with ideas, promotion, and undying support. Whatever success this book might achieve, I share with you as part of my soul.